Ten Differentiation Strategies for
Building Prior Knowledge

Jill Spencer

Association for Middle Level Education
Westerville, Ohio

Copyright © 2012 by the Association for Middle Level Education.

All rights reserved. No part of this publication may be reproduced or transmitted in any form or by any means, electronic or mechanical, without permission in writing from the publisher except in the case of brief quotations embodied in reviews or articles. The materials presented herein are the expressions of the author and do not necessarily represent the policies of the Association for Middle Level Education.

AMLE is a registered servicemark of the Association for Middle Level Education.

Printed in the United States of America.

ISBN: 978-1-56090-246-1

AMLE
Association for Middle Level Education
formerly National Middle School Association

Dedication

To Meghan Linn Hayes, Robyn Butler, and Kendall Morrison
Three beautiful little girls who bring me great joy!

Foreword

In this book, Jill Spencer shares her impressive experience as a classroom teacher; a coach of literacy, educational technology, pedagogy, and school change; and a middle level leader, author, and professional developer. The real beauty of this practical little book comes in the form of Jill's expert coaching. While she is explaining a Think Aloud with students, she is *doing* a Think Aloud with the reader—and helping you understand the thought processes you will go through to help your students connect what they already know to their next lesson. She shows you how to widen students' horizons, engage their interest, and pique their curiosity about the upcoming lesson or unit by making connections to what they already know. She gives you, the teacher, the building materials to successfully scaffold your lessons for your diverse learners.

Differentiation of instruction is more important today than ever before. Originally designed for the Industrial Age, schools of the past provided a basic education for all, developed the *talents of the few*, and promoted compliance of the rest. After all, we needed only a few business, military, political, and community leaders; but we needed a lot of factory workers, clerks, enlisted personnel, etc., who were good at what they were asked to do.

But today's Information Age workplace requires workers to be adaptive and constantly learning on the job. They must solve problems, think creatively, and bring a variety of skills to a variety of tasks. By necessity, then, the goal of an Information Age educational system has shifted to developing the *talents of all students*. If educating all students for the Industrial Age was a challenge, educating all students for the Information Age is an even greater challenge!

Teachers need strategies for identifying and building on students' diverse strengths. We need to differentiate in practical, manageable ways to tap into and leverage students' various approaches to learning and prepare them for their futures in the global community. A wide variety of content-based application examples and thorough directions for adapting the strategies for using digital tools make the oft-heard "Do I really have time to access prior knowledge?" question moot.

Jill's strategies are practical and concrete: read them today, use them in the classroom tomorrow. But don't expect them to be cut-and-dried: when you try these strategies you'll be fascinated by your students' responses and seriously engaged with them in taking what each of them knows about something to a new level. As they grow and stretch—as they have "aha" moments—so, too, will you. The information you get from students in these strategies adds many more arrows in your quiver as you find ways to help them develop into the best learners and people they can be.

Mike Muir, Ed. D.
Multiple Pathways Leader, Auburn School Department
Director, Maine Center for Meaningful Engaged Learning (www.mcmel.org)

Preface

I see them everywhere—in the grocery store, on TV, in the newspaper, on the street, even in the rolling credits of a Clint Eastwood movie. Thirty-plus years of students. Translated into real numbers, over 3,000 wonderful kids touched my life. I'm so very proud of them. They are entrepreneurs, lawyers, sales clerks, community activists, entertainers, lobstermen, parents, politicians, doctors, accountants, loggers, social workers, and teachers. However, some faces still haunt me, and I still worry about them. Every child did not find success in my classroom, and I continue to wonder what I should have or could have done differently to ensure they were more successful. *If only I had known, maybe I could have…* But, the past is gone, and I don't get any do-overs.

We can only go forward and work toward improving learning experiences for the present generation of students and those that follow. Improving instruction for young adolescents is my passion, and it is why I write. I am on a mission to share strategies and approaches, based in research, that I have learned from my own experiences and from observing and talking with marvelous educators across the country.

Differentiation is something I really wish I had understood as a young teacher. I was a liberal arts grad without any education background, and I believed that if I created wonderfully engaging and innovative lessons, my students would learn. Many did. Some did not, and *I didn't know what to do about it.* Plus, a few students were far more knowledgeable about certain topics than I was, and to tell the truth, I was a bit intimidated. And…*I didn't know what to do with them.* Those were the days of one-size-fits-all instruction, and too many students were left behind or bored.

Fortunately, over the past 35 years the research on how people learn has exploded, and educators have been able to apply this research in classrooms. We now understand that the brain makes connections between bits of information and that what students already know about a topic often predetermines how well they will master new information and skills. Hence, accessing and building prior knowledge is a critical element of any learning plan. We've also learned that reading issues are often not directly related to intelligence and that when we find ways for dyslexic students to access complex texts, they can discuss and respond to ideas in sophisticated ways. My goodness, we have even learned that intelligence is not a fixed commodity and can be improved through multiple exposures to intellectually stimulating experiences.

I am distressed by recent policies that promote a one-size-fits-all instructional approach despite the fact that there is much evidence that it rarely has long-term beneficial effects on one's learning. The adoption of the Common Core of State Standards with its rigid grade-level expectations will present educators with ongoing challenges. Fortunately, the recent research on formative assessment and the importance of feedback and early intervention identifies positive actions that can support students as they work to meet standards.

However, there will still be students who have advanced beyond their grade level academic standards in some areas, but not in others. Some students will still need additional help, while others fight personal demons that eat away at their motivation and perseverance. One-size-fits-all learning will never be the best solution to ensure that each student reaches his or her academic and personal potential; differentiation remains a critical, viable option that we need to incorporate into our thinking as we plan and implement the Common Core and other guiding principles of curriculum and instruction.

There is a major, recent advancement in teaching and learning that makes the promise of differentiation a reality, and that is technology. Digital tools and Internet resources provide teachers and students with multiple avenues for accessing information and demonstrating mastery and opportunities for collaborating with others around the world. When I visualize those faces of students whom I didn't reach, I always think, "Ah, if only you could have used text-to-speech capabilities; if only I could have connected you to an expert in the field; or if only you could have downloaded a video that you could watch multiple times, then maybe our time together would have better met your needs."

Whether using technology or more traditional strategies, differentiation is a complex process. When my AMLE editor, Carla Weiland, first suggested that I write about differentiation, I struggled with the organization and focus of the book. What did I have to say that Carol Ann Tomlinson or Rick Wormeli and others hadn't already said? Then Carla had the brilliant idea of breaking the topic of differentiation in general into a series of shorter books, each focusing on a particular aspect of instruction. *Ten Differentiation Strategies for Building Prior Knowledge* is hopefully the first in a series of books that highlight specific strategies to help teachers plan lessons and units addressing the learning needs and preferences of each of their students. Focusing just on the prior knowledge part of differentiation allows me to walk the reader through all the thought processes and application steps of each strategy.

Inspiration for my teaching and writing continues to come from my colleagues across Maine and now the nation. Whether I'm at the Sugarloaf Conference of the Maine Association for Middle Level Education, chatting on AMLE's MiddleTalk listserve, talking with teachers at the NELMS conference in Providence, or visiting a classroom in a distant state, I am always learning from my fellow educators. I thank them for their hard work and willingness to share ideas. My appreciation also goes to Carla Weiland and the publications staff at the Association for Middle Level Education. Their thoughtful editing and design ideas turn my ramblings and initial graphics into an attractive, coherent text.

Teaching is a wonderful way to spend one's life. It is intellectually challenging, emotionally fulfilling, and downright fun! Let's work together to keep the torch of learning burning bright—our students deserve the best we can offer.

Jill Spencer
Lisbon Falls, Maine
February 2012

Introduction

Teaching and learning are two complex processes. We hope that they are in perfect sync—what the teacher teaches, the student learns. But alas, that is not always the case. As a teacher I designate the learning targets, the curriculum materials I use, the instructional strategies I will employ, and how I will assess whether or not the students achieved mastery. I do not control the internal learning process of my students. I can use all of the resources I have to create optimal learning conditions; however, they are not a guarantee that each and every student will learn what I want them to learn. Therefore, I have to continually check for understanding and adapt my instructional plan as needed to help the students struggling with specific skills and knowledge. Adapting my instruction and curriculum materials to ensure each student has equitable access to a rich curriculum is one aspect of differentiation.

But first, before I finalize my overall teaching plan, I need to know my students' level of expertise related to the upcoming lesson or unit. Do they have the skills and knowledge I assume they have that are a necessary foundation for the new learning? How will I find out? What background knowledge would be helpful for all students to possess before we move forward? Do my students have any misconceptions based on past experiences that will get in the way of acquiring new knowledge? How will I uncover them? How will I correct them? Which students already have mastered the skills addressed and assessed in this lesson or unit? These questions all relate to accessing, building, and assessing prior knowledge, an extremely critical part of any instructional plan or curriculum unit.

Furthermore, if accessing, building, and assessing prior knowledge is so important, then I have to make sure to use strategies that engage every student. I need this information about my students' prior knowledge for 100% of my students. Yet I have a class full of students with specific learning needs, and I don't have the time to interview each and every one of them to find out what they already know. What can I do? The purpose of the book is to share 10 strategies that will help you access, build and/or assess prior knowledge in a differentiated manner so that you get the feedback you need to thoughtfully move forward in your planning.

Differentiation is a word that is bandied around as if educators, parents, and students all share the same definition. We don't! My favorite definition comes from Carol Ann Tomlinson and Caroline Cunningham Eidson in *Differentiation in Practice: A Resource Guide for Differentiating Curriculum* (2003):

> "...*differentiated instruction* refers to a systematic approach to planning curriculum and instruction for academically diverse learners. It is a way of thinking about a classroom with dual goals of honoring each student's learning needs and maximizing each student's learning capacity." (p. 3)

As the saying goes, the devil is in the details. What are the details we need to know about *learning needs* and *how to maximize learning capacity*? Fortunately, writers like Tomlinson, Wormeli, and Rakow address these issues extensively in their writings and presentations. They give concrete examples of designing units, using time strategically to orchestrate differentiation, and addressing cognitive differences. They help us internalize the principles of differentiation so that it becomes a natural extension of our lesson and unit planning.

However, there still remain competing state and national trends that complicate our thinking about differentiation. *The Common Core of State Standards* has *grade level specific* learning targets that will be assessed. Seventh graders will be expected to demonstrate mastery of skills and knowledge such as these.

- Determine the meaning of words and phrases as they are used in a text, including figurative and connotative meanings; analyze the impact of rhymes and other repetitions of sounds (e.g., alliteration) on a specific verse or stanza of a poem or section of a story or drama.
- Compute unit rates associated with ratios of fractions, including ratio of lengths, areas, and other quantities measured in like or different units.

The common core document is quite clear about expectations, *"Students advancing through the grades are expected to meet each year's grade-specific standards and retain or further develop skills and understandings mastered in preceding grades"* (Common Core of State Standards, 2010).

Meanwhile, there is also pressure to customize and personalize learning with time as an important variable—students do not always learn in lock-step sequence and manner on a rigid timeline. Larry Cuban (2012) in *Educational Leadership* quotes Jay McTighe and John Brown: "How can teachers address required content and grade-level performance standards while remaining responsive to individual students?" (p. 14). Cuban goes on to say that teachers make compromises.

Differentiation, despite the pressures for uniformity, continues to be a valid and effective way to approach teaching and learning that addresses the needs of the myriad diverse learners sitting in any one classroom. This book will be helpful to teachers in different circumstances:

- *For teachers who have the big picture of their next differentiated unit already in mind:* Here are 10 strategies to consider as you get down to the nitty-gritty of the specific day-to-day planning and are thinking about the ways to access, assess, or build prior knowledge.
- *For teachers who are just getting their toes wet in the differentiation ocean:* Here is a place to start to explore in a limited way (the beginning of the lesson) what differentiation looks like in practice.
- *For teachers who know they should incorporate accessing, assessing, or building prior knowledge in their lesson and units, but rarely do:* Here are a variety of different ways to increase the effectiveness of your lessons and units by building students' interest and gaining valuable information for yourself about what your students know and believe about a topic.
- *For teachers who just love to try new strategies:* Here are 10 strategies to adapt to your own classroom needs.
- *For teachers whose classrooms are fully engaged in the digital world:* Here are some traditional strategies that have been given a digital twist and some that only exist because of the power of the Internet and Web 2.0 tools.

The book opens with a short description of the importance of prior knowledge to learning and different ways to think about differentiation. Next are the detailed explanations of the 10 strategies. Each strategy has three classroom applications that from come from many different disciplines. The content examples certainly can be adapted to other types of classes or situations. They are designed to suggest possibilities, not as etched-in-stone examples.

Teaching and learning should be joyous processes. Classrooms should be filled with happily active students who create, debate, and collaborate as they work diligently to master important skills and knowledge. Hopefully, readers will find an approach or two they can use to initiate lessons and units in a way that gives them critical information they need about their students' prior knowledge while engaging their students in thoughtful consideration of the upcoming topics.

Contents

Foreword..**v**
Preface..**vii**
Introduction..**xi**

Part One: Four Ways to Differentiate **1**
Attributes of Learners...**5**
Learning Differences/Needs **7**
Gender Differences...**8**
Background Knowledge and Concrete/Abstract Thinking Continuum **10**

Part Two: FAQs about Prior Knowledge **15**
1. What are four reasons for accessing and/or building prior knowledge of a lesson or unit topic?...**17**
2. What are the characteristics of evidence-based strategies that effectively build students' prior knowledge?..**18**
3. What if I don't have time for activating prior knowledge activities?.....**19**
4. What are some strategies to differentiate prior knowledge activities?...**19**

Part Three: Ten Strategies for Activating, Building, and Assessing Prior Knowledge...**23**
1 Anticipatory Guide **25**
2 At the Mall **35**

3	Expanded KWL Using an Article or Film Clip	**43**
4	Carousel	**53**
5	Children's Picture Books	**63**
6	Podcasts	**75**
7	Skits and other Kinesthetic Activities	**87**
8	Slideshows and Videos	**99**
9	Student-Generated Webs	**109**
10	Word Sorts	**119**

Appendix **131**
References **149**

Part One

Four Ways to Differentiate

Four Ways to Differentiate

Differentiation of instruction is complex. Teachers must be knowledgeable about:
- Students' individual learning needs.
- Content.
- Appropriate state and national standards.
- Varied assessment tools.
- Applying data to classroom instruction.
- Learning theory.
- Multiple instructional strategies.

An overarching framework that makes sense of all of these elements is Universal Design for Learning, known by its acronym, UDL. This model organizes differentiation goals into three categories. Differentiation should:
- Present information and content in different ways so that everyone has access to a high quality curriculum.
- Allow students to demonstrate their learning in multiple ways.
- Engage students in learning by stimulating their interests and motivation.

UDL includes the three most common entry points for differentiating mentioned in professional development workshops, articles, websites, and books:
- content (what is taught)
- process (how information is learned)
- product (how students demonstrate mastery)

The Center for Applied Special Technologies (CAST), a non-profit research and development organization, has a useful website about UDL (http://www.cast.org/).

Beyond the overarching framework and entry points are the instructional strategies teachers employ to meet the goals of differentiation. There are multiple ways to differentiate: readiness, pacing, learning styles, sight and hearing needs, gender consideration, cognitive development, student interest, motivation, methods of processing information, literacy skills, etc. Fortunately, it is possible to group or categorize the different ways to address the diverse learning needs of students in any given classroom.

By organizing student needs, a teacher can think systematically about differentiation instead of using a scatter-shot approach. Below is a chart that explains the organization of the practices described in this book. Following it are more in-depth discussions of these categories.

\	Differentiation Practices
Category	**Some things to consider**
Attributes of Learners	• Learning styles (visual. auditory, kinesthetic, logical, mathematical, literary, interpersonal, digital) • Gardiner's multiple intelligences • Internal and social processing
Learning Differences/ Needs	• Special education Individual Education Plans (IEPs) • Advanced learners' needs • Reading readiness and other literacy issues • 504 plans • Universal Design for Learning
Gender Differences	• Kinesthetic experiences • Peer collaboration
Background Knowledge and Concrete to Abstract Thinking Continuum	• Experiences and vocabulary students bring to the classroom • Levels of sophistication in the development of cognitive structures (comparative thinking, symbolic representation, logical reasoning) • Time of development of abstract thinking

Attributes of Learners

Buyer Beware! These two words offer a cautionary tale when we think about differentiating through learning styles and multiple intelligences. Many educators accept as undisputed fact that students' learning styles and multiple intelligence profiles hold the key to increasing learning and achievement. Books, articles and presentations abound about the application of these two theories to curriculum and instruction. However, there is a spirited debate among educational theorists, cognitive psychologists, and others about the validity of these two theories and their application to the classroom.

Both theories are appealing because they parallel many educators' experiences in the classroom. Students do respond differently to various lesson formats. They do have different strengths that can often be characterized by labels such as visual, auditory, interpersonal, logical, and mathematical. The crux of the matter seems to be whether or not teaching specific content through these strengths increases learning. Daniel Willingham, a cognitive psychologist from the University of Virginia, states the research "provides substantial evidence that tailoring instruction to students' modality is not effective (Willingham, 2005). The late Rita Dunn who was a professor at St. John's University and a leading proponent of learning styles theory disagreed and cited other research (Dunn, 1990). Similar differences of opinion swirl around the application of Gardiner's Multiple Intelligence Theory to classroom practice (Armstrong, 2009).

In light of the conflicting evidence, what's a teacher to do?

- *Research.* First, do a little research on the topic. If you are a staunch supporter of using learning styles in your instruction, read what the critics have to say and think through your responses to their main points. In this day of easy access to information, someone will eventually challenge you in a meeting or a conference with an article by Willingham or another critic. It is crucial that teachers are able to articulate why their choice of pedagogical practices is effective and how it will benefit individual students.

- *Seek commonalities.* Secondly, look for commonalities in conflicting points of view. For example, Willingham maintains, "Teachers should focus on the content's best modality—not the student's" (2005). In other words, if you are teaching the characteristics of the different types of triangles, it is important to include visuals of them for all students. Even students with strong auditory or kinesthetic abilities need to see the images of the triangles. Hoping to help their visual learners understand the concept, teachers using the traditional learning styles approach would also include visuals.

Critics of teaching to student learning styles are not suggesting that all instruction should be the same for every topic during the entire class period. Instead, they maintain that decisions should be grounded in good instructional practices that help students internalize the new information. They are convinced, however, that teaching a visual concept through an auditory approach or teaching a kinesthetic move, such as pitching a softball, solely through a visual strategy to address learning styles is not good pedagogy. No one will disagree with the notion that all instruction should be based in effective instructional practice. The term "evidence-based" is currently in vogue for describing such strategies. Whether you are an avid proponent of learning styles theory or a skeptic, you should develop an instructional plan embracing strategies proven to work.

- *Never underestimate the power of novelty.* As Muir points out in his Meaningful Engaged Learning model, novelty piques student interest in a subject (2001). Willingham, the sharp critic of learning styles, writes, "… as experienced teachers know, a change in modality can provide a welcome change of pace that brings students' attention back to a lesson" (2005). Changing the method of delivery of information during a lesson will engage students' attention because it breaks routine, and it may play to students' different learning strengths.

- *Digital learning style?* I wonder about adding a category of digital learning style. In the mid-1990s, I was in the library with my class working on a research project. Back then, the library had a bank of six desktop computers with access to the Internet, and I thought that we were in high-tech heaven. Although students had to take turns using the computers, a wide range of reference books provided ample references for the project. Jacob, a smart, charming eighth grader, was chatting at a table, and I suggested he might want to use his time wisely. "I'm waiting to use a computer," he replied. When I reminded him of all the print options, he looked at me seriously and said, "I'm just not into turning those paper pages." That comment was my first real signal that this generation accessed information much differently than I did. Fifteen years later, I think I've caught up with Jacob and other digital natives—I don't turn paper pages any more when I do research, and I read and make notations in books on my iPad. Today's students use their visual and auditory strengths plus their dexterity in keying with just their thumbs to accomplish all sorts of tasks. To honor these digital natives' learning needs, we will address learning digitally as well.

For the purposes of this book, I will use *learning attributes* as an inclusive term embracing the ideas of the proponents and critics of learning styles, the multiple intelligence theories of Gardiner, and the needs of the digital learner.

Learning Differences/Needs

Special education accommodations and modifications, 504 plans, personalized learning for gifted and talented students, and short-term needs presented by students with an illness, injury, or travel plans require the teacher to be a nimble thinker when crafting lesson plans. The definition for Universal Design for Learning on the CAST website perhaps best defines this category of differentiation:

> Universal Design for Learning is a set of principles for curriculum development that gives all individuals equal opportunities to learn.

Ensuring equity. Equal opportunities to learn and have equal access to a rich and challenging curriculum—these are the outcomes for any differentiation initiative. As many writers have stated, differentiation is a state of mind rather than a set of strategies. The teacher is always thinking about content, process, and products and ways to structure them to ensure equity in the classroom. This state of mind also includes an understanding that reading problems or difficulty with expressive language or physical impairment do not mean that intellect is lacking.

Accessing content in multiple ways has become easier in the digital age. Videos, podcasts, digital textbooks, and text-to-speech applications are readily available alternatives to traditional textbooks. Furthermore, digital devices also give students multiple ways to demonstrate their mastery of new learning. Finally, the standards approach to curriculum makes transparent what students should know and be able to do. This clarity of purpose helps to focus what elements of a lesson or unit the teacher needs to differentiate.

Scaffolding. Scaffolding is another major component of differentiating for learning differences and needs. *"In scaffolding instruction a more knowledgeable 'other' provides scaffolds or supports to facilitate the learner's development. The scaffolds facilitate a student's ability to build on prior knowledge and internalize new information" (Van Der Stuyf, 2002).*

The term "scaffolding" is taken from the field of construction where carpenters build steel or wooden frameworks to support them while they work on projects. Instructional scaffolding simply means building supports into the learning activity to model how thinking processes work, giving students non-threatening practices to help them develop these thought processes, and then having them apply the processes to an assignment.

Scaffolding strategies include:
- Breaking the tasks into chunks.
- Providing images, text, and auditory delivery of information.
- Accessing and connecting to participants' prior knowledge.
- Keeping the atmosphere psychologically and physically safe.
- Providing opportunities to try out ideas and revise them without fear of failure.
- Using groups to generate ideas so no one is left out of the activity.
- Modeling the thinking involved in the task.
- Using writing frames.
- Modeling thinking, reading, or writing strategies through Think Alouds.

A variety of state and federal statutes provide for the learning needs of all students. More importantly, it is a moral imperative for educators to ensure each student has equal access to the curriculum they need to live productively in the 21st century.

Gender Differences

The role of gender differences in learning and achievement is receiving a great deal of attention. Statistics from tests such as the National Assessment of Educational Progress (NAEP) are used to build the case that boys are at a disadvantage in schools. Similar to the various opinions about the usefulness of addressing learning styles to raise student achievement, researchers and authors also differ widely in their interpretation of recent brain research findings on male and female brains and their relationship to teaching and learning.

In a 2010 issue of *Educational Leadership* focused on the theme of closing opportunity gaps, the different points of view are obvious. Lise Eliot, associate professor of neuroscience at the Chicago Medical School of Rosalind Franklin University, states in the article

"The Myth of Pink and Blue Brains": "The truth is that neuroscientists have identified very few reliable differences between boys' and girls' brains" (p. 32). The authors of "Gender-Friendly Schools", on the other hand, point to specific differences in the brain's right hemisphere, frontal lobe development, and neural rest states that they feel impact learning (p. 41). These two articles are just one example of the ongoing argument.

Kathleen Cleveland in *Teaching Boys Who Struggle in School* distills the arguments of the two sides into these perspectives (p. 6):

1. Today's classrooms, pedagogies, and teachers favor girls. Boys' brains are hardwired to require a different kind of learning than girls' brains do.
2. There is a wide variation among individuals of the same sex. It is inappropriate to draw causal links between observations about brain structure or activity and human behavior.

Cleveland thinks that both positions fall short by perhaps being too broad. She found that generalizations about gender differences were not sufficient because "…problems [among students] were unique, and the solutions to those problems must necessarily be unique as well (p. 8). Sweeping decisions and actions may not address the learning needs of specific individuals, no matter their gender. So once again, teachers and administrators should explore both sides of the debate before committing to any radical changes in organization, curriculum, and instruction. There has been a lot written on this topic, so it pays to understand the different perspectives and to have solid reasons behind any decisions affecting children.

The good news, however, is that there are commonalities among the different interpretations of research on adolescent brain development and its effects on how boys and girls learn. These shared understandings will help educators think about their curriculum and instruction in terms of differentiation. Below is a list of things to consider suggested by these *Educational Leadership* authors and others.

- There is a large variation across both sexes in how individuals learn. Therefore, it is very important not to stereotype boys or girls as specific types of learners.
- The way we bring up our children does impact their learning in school.
    - Spatial intelligence and visual learning are important to nurture, perhaps especially in girls, who often don't engage in this type of learning outside of school. These skills are important in a variety of subjects including advanced math and science.

- Boys really need to be immersed in words—reading, writing, and vocabulary development.
- Active learning strategies benefit most students.
- Student choice and interest engage students in the learning process.

Middle level educators recognize these characteristics of gender-sensitive teaching as effective instructional practices at the middle level.

Background Knowledge and Concrete to Abstract Thinking Continuum

New information has to connect to something already known if the learner is to successfully internalize it. "To store all the data usefully, our brains organize material into networks based on conceptual categories. Your memory of how to use an eggbeater is probably linked to your knowledge of other kitchen utensils, memories of particular recipes, recollections of learning to cook, and so on" (Squire, 2007). This process is called consolidation.

In the opening pages of *Building Background Knowledge for Academic Achievement*, Marzano (2004) states, "…the research literature supports one compelling fact: what students *already know* about the content is one of the strongest indicators of how well they will learn new information relative to the content" (p. 1).

One of the major findings of the authors of *How People Learn: Brain, Mind, Experience, and School* (2006) is

> "Students come to the classroom with preconceptions about how the world works. If their initial understanding is not engaged, they may fail to grasp the new concepts and information that are taught, or they may learn them for purposes of a test but revert to their preconceptions outside of the classroom." (p. 15)

Obviously, students' prior experiences and knowledge play a major role in their academic work. Any group of 25 youngsters is going to have a wide range of familiarity with the topic about to be studied, and the teacher needs to learn what experiences her students have had relative to the content they will study. Before the unit begins she can fill in any foundational gaps of knowledge and build on students' prior experiences during the unit.

Background knowledge example. Think about starting a geography unit requiring students to identify geographical features such as buttes, bays, and bayous. In the class there are students from military families who have lived all over the country and perhaps the world, students whose families visit a different national park every summer, and students who have never been ten miles away from their coastal homes. Some of the students have stood at the base of Bear Butte in South Dakota and craned their necks to stare up at its towering majesty. They have a vivid image in their minds of a butte and will relate that image to anything they read about the geographical landform called a butte. Others, having never traveled beyond the rolling hills and relatively gentle mountains of New England, might read "Bear Butte" in their text and hear in their minds "Bear Butt". Two totally different learning experiences! Which student is easily going to internalize the characteristics of buttes? Attending to the varied background knowledge of students is a critical aspect of differentiation.

Abstract Thinking. Just as there is a big discrepancy in young adolescents' background knowledge, there are also major inconsistencies in their development of abstract thinking skills. Moving along the continuum of concrete to abstract thinking ability is a different journey for each individual. This journey begins in the middle grades, but does not necessarily end there. Piaget and other developmental psychologists tell us that abstract thinking is defined as formal operational thinking composed of the ability to:

- Understand abstractions.
- Develop hypotheses.
- Problem solve in a systematic way.
- Develop conceptual thinking.

If cognitive development were a lockstep procedure, it would be much simpler for the teacher. *A child turns twelve and magically understands the processes of analysis. In the thirteenth year they learn how to evaluate a situation and make a rational decision based on the data they have accumulated.* But alas, this is not so. Some eleven-year-olds are able to think more abstractly than their thirteen-year-old schoolmates. Some days it seems your seventh grade science students have all internalized the concept of hypothesis, and the next day it seems they have never before heard the word. Cognitive development is a bumpy road.

Bloom's Taxonomy. Directed to ensure lessons incorporate critical thinking, teachers often use Bloom's Taxonomy as a guide for planning their lessons. The original taxonomy of the 1950s includes the categories of knowledge, comprehension, application, analysis, evaluation and synthesis. The 1990 version, which Lorin Anderson was instrumental in revising, includes remembering, understanding, applying, analyzing, evaluating, and creating. Many of the elements in both versions of the taxonomy fall into the category of formal operations. Advocates of 21st century skills also call for critical thinking and problem-solving skills.

Is there a total disconnect between current curricular demands for higher level thinking skills and middle grades students' cognitive development? No! However, the savvy teacher must be aware of where her students are along the continuum of concrete thinking to operational/abstract thinking and differentiate appropriately to ensure students are able to successfully complete a task and follow through on a process. Modeling for students the specific steps in thinking processes before, during, and after a lesson is an example of scaffolding, a key differentiation strategy that benefits all students. For example, if a science teacher were going to ask students to evaluate the effectiveness of different alternative energy resources as solutions to the United States' dependence on foreign oil, he would want to make sure students knew how to make judgments based on evidence rather than feelings. He might choose to use an example such as this one from *Everyone's Invited! Interactive Strategies That Engage Young Adolescents* (2008) to model the process students should use as they evaluate energy alternatives.

Once the students have practiced this process for evaluating, they can apply it to an assignment. It might be a project on the most effective president in the 20th century, the best sources of energy for the 21st century, or the most imaginative author of fantasy novels for teens. Students who are still basically concrete thinkers do not have to be doomed to endless worksheets; they can problem solve, synthesize, and evaluate if they are taught how to use thinking strategies *before* they are assigned the critical thinking task.

Example Strategy for Teacher to Model the Thinking Process of "Evaluation"

Steps

- Share a student-friendly definition of evaluation:
  "To examine something carefully in order to judge its worth or value."
- List key words that alert students when they are being asked to evaluate:
  assess, determine, justify, choose, select, verify, rank, or judge.
- Explain that there are multiple ways to evaluate and give examples:
    - *Create criteria to use to judge the value (make a chart).*
    - *Compare to another similar idea or object and determine which is better.*
    - *Make a choice and back it up with specific reasons.*
- Model one strategy with a Think Aloud and then invite the students to participate:

    Think Aloud example: *Lots of times in your life, you are going to have to evaluate a situation or a potential purchase and decide which provides you with the best value—financial, emotional, intellectual, etc. We are going to explore a process you can use in a multitude of situations in which you use criteria, compare items according to those criteria, and leave with reasons to back up your decision. We're going to create a matrix, and we are going to evaluate music groups—bet you all have an opinion on that topic! Let me model what I mean about criteria—concert tickets cost big bucks, so before I'm willing to spend that kind of money, the group has to meet my criteria. My criteria are that I have to: recognize the songs; be able to sing along; be able to make a comment to a friend without shouting; and I want to leave the show humming. So—the Kingston Trio, Manhattan Transfer, and Bob Dylan all fit my criteria.* **Hint: obviously any criteria and groups can be used in the Think Aloud—the point is for the students to see and hear the process**.

    When you stop laughing at my criteria, you can have a go at deciding which band is best. But instead of trying to shout each other down, you will be able to build a case with evidence to support your stand. With a partner, work through the process of developing a criteria matrix. Maybe we had better make sure everyone knows what criteria are—who can define that word for us?

- Students work together to decide on common criteria for judging their favorite groups.
- They fill in criteria across the top of a matrix and then list the groups down its left side. See a matrix example on the next page.
- Individually, they rank the groups on a scale of 1 to 3 for each criterion.
- They complete the matrix by adding and recording the totals.

Figure 1-1 *Example of Criteria Matrix*

Example of Criteria Matrix				
Group	Criteria			Total Points
	Lyrics	Band Personality	Appropriate for dancing to	
Beatles				
Rolling Stones				

Part Two

FAQs About Prior Knowledge

FAQs About Prior Knowledge

1. **What are four reasons for accessing and/or building students' prior knowledge of a lesson or unit topic?**

First, we internalize new knowledge by connecting it to something we already know. A toddler begins to conceptualize "cat" by stroking its fur. Mom or dad says, "Soft cat," and the child connects the word "cat" and the feel of its fur. Then, the cat meows, and another association is made with this thing that feels soft. The associations accumulate until the toddler has internalized that this four-legged critter that feels soft, makes several sounds, and will scratch if its tail is pulled is a cat. Eventually, the child will learn not only to say "cat," but also to spell the word.

The same process occurs as we learn new things in school. We connect what we need to learn by comparing and contrasting it to things we already know. Consider geographic landforms. "Mountain" is a fairly easy word to learn and visualize. We learn the word "plateau" by picturing a mountain with its top cut off. Once a student has internalized plateau, she can connect that image with the term "escarpment," the steep leading edge of a plateau. If the student can't visualize a plateau, then the term "escarpment" will probably be forgotten.

When planning a lesson or unit, a teacher must identify what prior knowledge and skills students need to make connections to the new content, assess whether or not students possess that knowledge, and if they don't, figure out how to build it.

Secondly, it is imperative for teachers to identify any misconceptions related to the upcoming lesson or unit. In a famous old video filmed at an Ivy League university graduation, an interviewer asked the new graduates to explain why there are seasons.

Many of the responses were inaccurate. Somewhere along the line, these graduates had internalized a misconception about the relationship of the earth to the sun, and it never changed during their 16 years of intense education. A misconception can be as simple as "every s at the end of a word deserves an apostrophe" to a life-threatening belief about electricity and conductivity. Long-held misconceptions block the internalization of new, accurate information that a person needs to make decisions or understand additional complex ideas. Unfortunately, just presenting evidence that corrects an erroneous understanding of a concept or event is not enough to rectify the misconception in students' minds. Because students have to unlearn bad information or incorrect processes, teachers must pinpoint exactly what the misconceptions are and plan accordingly.

Related to reasons one and two is the fact that teachers cannot properly plan a lesson or a unit without knowing who knows what! No one wants to teach ideas, concepts, or skills students have already mastered, or to make an assumption that everyone in the class possesses specific knowledge and skills. Activating and assessing prior knowledge gives the teacher the necessary information to differentiate during the unit, especially in the areas of content and process.

A fourth reason to build in time to assess and build prior knowledge is that the process can and should hook students into wanting to know more. An effective strategy will engage the students in asking questions and wondering why and how. Building anticipation for what comes next is important, and searching for the why and how pulls the students into the learning.

2. What are the characteristics of evidence-based strategies that effectively build students' prior knowledge?

Christen and Murphy (1991) suggest several ways to build student prior knowledge:
- Pre-teach vocabulary.
- Enrich their background knowledge.
- Help students develop their own conceptual framework so they can continue to build background knowledge independently.

3. What if I don't have time for activating prior knowledge activities?

Because they believe there isn't enough time to include such activities, teachers often skip activating and assessing students' prior knowledge. However, if the time isn't spent up front, it will be spent on the tail end of a lesson or unit when students cannot demonstrate mastery. There will be a variety of reasons why students are unsuccessful. A misconception might be the culprit that blocks understanding, or perhaps the student is unable to apply the new learning because it's hanging out there in space and connected to nothing. Frustration on both the teacher and students' parts when learning does not occur leads to a less-than-positive classroom climate. Take the time upfront to assess and build background knowledge!

A follow-up question might be: *How much time?* There is no easy answer to this question. If the upcoming lesson is simple in nature, the portion related to accessing/ building/ assessing prior knowledge might only be 10 or 15 minutes. However, if the forthcoming unit lessons are complex, rely on prerequisite knowledge, or are abstract in nature, then an entire class session or two may be necessary. There is no formula, and this type of decision is when the teacher's experience, prior knowledge, and understanding of the developmental needs of young adolescents come into play. It is better to err on the side of spending a bit more time than necessary than skimping on this process.

4. What are some strategies to differentiate prior knowledge activities?

The chart below lists multiple purposes for differentiating and the student needs and preferences they target. These needs and preferences are divided into the four general differentiation categories described previously:

- Attributes of learners
- Learning differences and needs
- Gender differences
- Background knowledge and concrete-to-abstract thinking continuum

The other column of the chart lists several strategies described in the book specifically addressing each need and preference. Any of the book's ten strategies can be adapted to address specific differentiation purposes; however, this chart provides a starting place for the reader. Both the data the teacher gathers from these strategies and the basic knowledge students gain work to increase the effectiveness of the ensuing lesson or unit.

Differentiation Strategies Targeted to Meet Specific Student Needs

Learning Attributes	Strategies
Wants to understand the relevance of a lesson	Anticipatory Guide
Feels comfortable with text	Anticipatory Guide, Expanded KWL, Children's Books
Prefers to think out loud to process ideas	Anticipatory Guide, At the Mall, Carousel, Word Sorts
Requires quiet "think time"	Anticipatory Guide, Podcasts, Student-Generated Webs
Is a digital learner	Digital Carousel, Expanded KWL, Podcasts, Slide Shows and Videos
Helped by visuals	Children's Books, Skits and other Kinesthetic Activities, Slide Shows and Videos, Student-Generated Webs, Word Sorts
Helped by combination of visual and audio formats	Podcasts, Skits and other Kinesthetic Activities, Slide Shows and Videos
Motivated by connecting learning to interests	All strategies
Motivated by incorporating student questions	All strategies
Learning Differences/Needs	
Needs cues to identify big ideas	Anticipatory Guide, At the Mall, Carousel
Needs key words identified	Children's Books, Slide Shows and Videos, Word Sorts
Is English language learner (ELL)	Children's Books, Carousel, Slide Shows and Videos

Reads below grade level	Children's Books, Expanded KWL, Podcasts
Learns at advanced levels	Expanded KWL, Podcasts
Requires multiple exposures to text, video, explanations, etc.	At the Mall, Podcasts, Slide Shows and Videos
Requires alternative ways to demonstrate knowledge	Skits and Other Kinesthetic Activities, Student-Generated Webs
Needs prompts to retrieve words and concepts	Carousel, Expanded KWL, Word Sorts
Requires alternatives or scaffolding for writing tasks	Carousel, Student-Generated Webs
Gender Differences	
Prefers working alone	Anticipatory Guide, Podcasts, Student-Generated Webs
Needs movement and other kinesthetic activity to learn well	Carousel, Skits and Other Kinesthetic Activities
Prefers group work	At the Mall, Carousel, Word Sorts
Concrete-Abstract Thinking Continuum	
Needs to connect vocabulary and concept to concrete examples	Children's Books, Skits and Other Kinesthetic Activities, Slide Shows and Videos
Background Knowledge	
Lacks background information/skills	Children's Books, Expanded KWL, Slide Shows and Videos
Needs to build academic vocabulary	At the Mall, Children's Books, Podcasts, Word Sorts

In the following section each of the ten strategies is described in detail.

1. A short **description** of the strategy as it looks in action helps you visualize its strengths and helps you begin thinking of how you might adapt it for your own classroom.

2. The **purpose** of the strategy indicates its different functions and strengths; not every strategy works for every topic.

3. **How the strategy differentiates** explains which students will benefit from each particular strategy.

4. **Procedures** for teachers provide some guidelines. Feel free to experiment and adapt strategies to meet your students' needs.

5. **Several content examples** show specific classroom scenarios of how teachers of different content areas might apply the strategy. I have explained why a teacher might use it in this particular way. Not meant as cookie-cutter lessons to be transferred as written to a particular lesson or unit, the examples are catalysts for fine-tuning lessons and units. The goal is to provide examples across the curriculum, but all of the strategies can be adapted in myriad ways to all subject areas. Your adaptations may prove to be improvements on the original idea! It never works to try to exactly superimpose a strategy into one's own classroom.

Note that activities designed to activate, build, or assess prior knowledge usually do not include long reading passages, projects, lengthy writings, or multi-media assignments. Therefore, some very traditional differentiation strategies associated with these activities do not appear in the descriptions that follow. We will not be discussing multiple products, rubrics, tiered curriculum, or multiple texts. Despite not using these strategies, there are still myriad ways to differentiate so that each student feels invited to the lesson and has a degree of confidence that he or she can be successful.

Part Three

Ten Strategies for Activating, Building, and Assessing Prior Knowledge

Anticipatory Guide

Description

This strategy engages students in thinking about the big ideas or concepts contained in a text or video before they read or view it. When students are provided with intriguing or provocative statements to ponder, they access their own prior knowledge and perceptions to connect with the information they are about to read or view. Additionally, anticipatory guides provide the teacher with information about student background knowledge and any misperceptions they have about the upcoming topic.

The strategy begins with students responding individually or in pairs to a series of statements or questions that capture the big ideas or concepts of the forthcoming text or video assignment. The responses are usually in the form of true/false or agree/disagree forced choices. After students have responded to the prompts, the teacher holds a full class or small group discussion period. Then the class reads or views the assignment. When they begin to read or view the video, students are focused on the important ideas and look for validation of their points of view. To connect the ideas discussed during the prior knowledge segment of the lesson to the information students have learned by the end of the unit, it often makes sense for students to go back to the anticipatory guide and reflect on how their initial responses have changed.

Anticipatory guide questions or statements often appear deceptively simple to answer, yet when students begin to read the guide, they find the issues have more facets than they had anticipated. For example, an anticipatory guide statement about an energy unit reads: "Green energy resources do not harm the environment." Although many students will agree, further guide references to bird and bat kills by wind turbines and questions about the safety of hybrid car batteries foreshadow the complexity of the topic. Because they are already thinking about issues raised by the guide and ensuing discussions, they are primed to mentally interact with the text or video, an important step in comprehending new information.

Although crafting questions and statements that connect to critical ideas and are relevant to students is important when creating an anticipatory guide, you might also find using humor an effective strategy. Humor's novel and/or out-of-context approach can capture students' attention and help them remember the important issues that were connected to the humor. A math example of such a guide question is: "Pi is the ratio of a circle's circumference to its diameter and comes in the flavors of apple, lemon meringue, and chocolate cream."

Purpose

- Ascertain the level of prior knowledge so the teacher can plan effectively
- Engage students in thinking about major concepts in an upcoming assignment
- Build interest and elicit student questions
- Encourage students to read text or watch a video closely and to seek out details that validate or contradict their thinking
- Provide scaffolding for learners who have difficulties identifying the main ideas
- Use as a starting point of discussion

How It Differentiates

- Appeals to students who feel comfortable with text
- Allows students who prefer thinking out loud to process ideas orally
- Allows students who prefer working alone to have that opportunity
- Provides cues to guide less able readers when they read independently
- Addresses the different speeds at which students process information
- Provides the teacher with an opportunity to cluster gifted and talented students to discuss ideas more intensely

Procedure for Teacher

1. Pre-read the text, view the video, or review the presentation to identify the major concepts and ideas you want your students to understand.
2. Create a guide similar to the one below by writing statements or questions based on these major points. Often the statements are written in true/false format or with a Likert Scale *(strongly disagree, disagree, agree, strongly agree)*. Including a question or two similar to number 3 makes the concepts to be studied relevant to students because it asks for a response based on personal experience or belief.

True/False Anticipatory Guide		
Directions: Before reading the assignment, read each of the following statements and check off the ones you think are true. After reading the assignment, reread the statements, and check off the ones you think are true.		
Before Reading	After Reading	
1. ☐	☐	The people in the Abolitionist Movement were determined to wipe out slavery.
2. ☐	☐	The abolitionists were pretty much all New Englanders.
3. ☐	☐	If your cause is just, sometimes you might have to resort to violence in order to further your cause.

3. There are a couple of ways to proceed after identifying the key ideas to include in the guide. The next decision is how to engage the students in responding to the questions:

    - Give each student a handout to complete individually.
    - Use a free digital survey tool such as Survey Monkey (see Appendix) to elicit student responses.
    - Put the questions up on a screen and have students respond with clickers (see Appendix).
    - Place charts (consensograms) with the prompts around the room and have students use colored sticky dots to respond via a Likert scale.

Figure 1.1 Consensogram

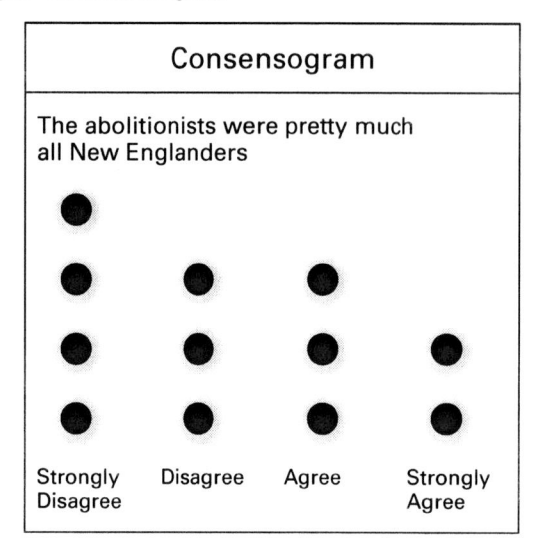

Consensogram

The abolitionists were pretty much all New Englanders

| Strongly Disagree | Disagree | Agree | Strongly Agree |

4. The next decision is how to process the guides with the students:

- Put students into small groups to discuss answers and report out information they all agreed on and questions they have.

- Consensograms and digital surveys make the data visible to everyone. Use questions such as

    – What do you notice?

    – What surprises you?

    – What additional information do we need?

You must have a poker face during these proceedings. The point is to gather information on student understandings and confusions, not to be dispensing information. It's also a great time to probe student thinking with comments such as:

- Please talk a little bit more about that idea.

- What do these questions/statements make you wonder about?

- In what ways can you connect this information to something we have already studied?

5. Now it's show time. Students have experienced the previews of coming attractions through the guide and ensuing conversations. They are primed to read, view, or listen to find out if their suppositions are correct. Everyone likes to be proven right! Proceed with the lesson.

6. Return to the anticipatory guide and have students record their responses after reading, viewing, or listening. In small groups or with the entire class, review the changes in answers and discuss the implications.

Content Examples

Social studies: Mrs. Washington's current unit focuses on the time period just prior to the American Civil War. The topic is abolition, including John Brown's raid on Harpers Ferry. Her students received a longer version of the anticipatory guide shown earlier.

- Mrs. Washington pre-taught the words "abolition" and "abolitionist."
- Individually, students fill in the guide and then work with a partner to compare answers and formulate questions.
- A whole-class discussion ensues as partners share their observations and questions which Mrs. Washington records as guides for the students to use during reading.

The segment of the lesson focusing on prior knowledge ends with a discussion centering on the last statement in the anticipatory guide, "If your cause is just, sometimes you might have to resort to violence in order to further your cause." Mrs. Washington asks students to connect this sentiment with what's going on in the world today. Naturally, she reminds students of their discussion guidelines because contemporary issues sometimes draw out passionate responses, and it's important to remain respectful when disagreements arise.

Her purpose in using an anticipatory guide is threefold: (1) check for understanding of the two words just taught, (2) help her less able readers set a specific purpose for reading, and (3) build interest in the topic. She recognizes that a number of students process information in a deliberative fashion, so she provides individual think time. There are also a number of students who engage by talking about ideas, so working with a partner will address their learning strengths.

Science: The seventh grade science class is about to begin a unit on energy. Mr. Bernard is interested in finding out two things: What knowledge do the students possess about the different types of energy available in the U.S.? What misperceptions exist? He also wants to generate some "energy" for this unit and encourage his students to start asking insightful questions about energy production and use in the U.S. and the world. These questions will eventually lead to a research project. He has also been reading about gender differences in learning. Despite the fact that there is a difference of opinion on the science surrounding gender differences in learning, most everyone agrees that incorporating movement into the instructional plan benefits boys. Therefore, he is going to use a consensogram for the anticipatory guide because students move to the charts to respond. Everyone will get a stretch before class discussion time. The charts also serve as strong visuals, allowing everyone to see the class's opinions on some provocative questions.

When the students first enter the classroom, they each receive four sticky dots. Going to each chart, they place one sticky dot over the response *(strongly disagree, disagree, agree. strongly agree)* that best captures their opinion. When the class is done, the charts look like the ones on the following page.

Mr. Bernard then leads a data discussion:
- What do you notice?
- What surprises you?
- What other information do we need to respond to these statements with assurance?
- What questions do we need to ask?
- What vocabulary words do we need to make sure we understand?

As he is recording the students' responses on the class wiki (see Appendix), he makes mental notes about misconceptions he hears so that he can address them directly. Mr. B. then leads the class through a process of organizing all their questions into categories, so they can begin the process of writing essential questions that later will guide their inquiry projects. The student generation of questions will help him differentiate by interest in the next segment of the unit. He is also providing practice in critical thinking skills—looking for logical ways to group the questions builds students' ability to look for organizing principles.

Figure 1.2 Class Consensograms on Energy

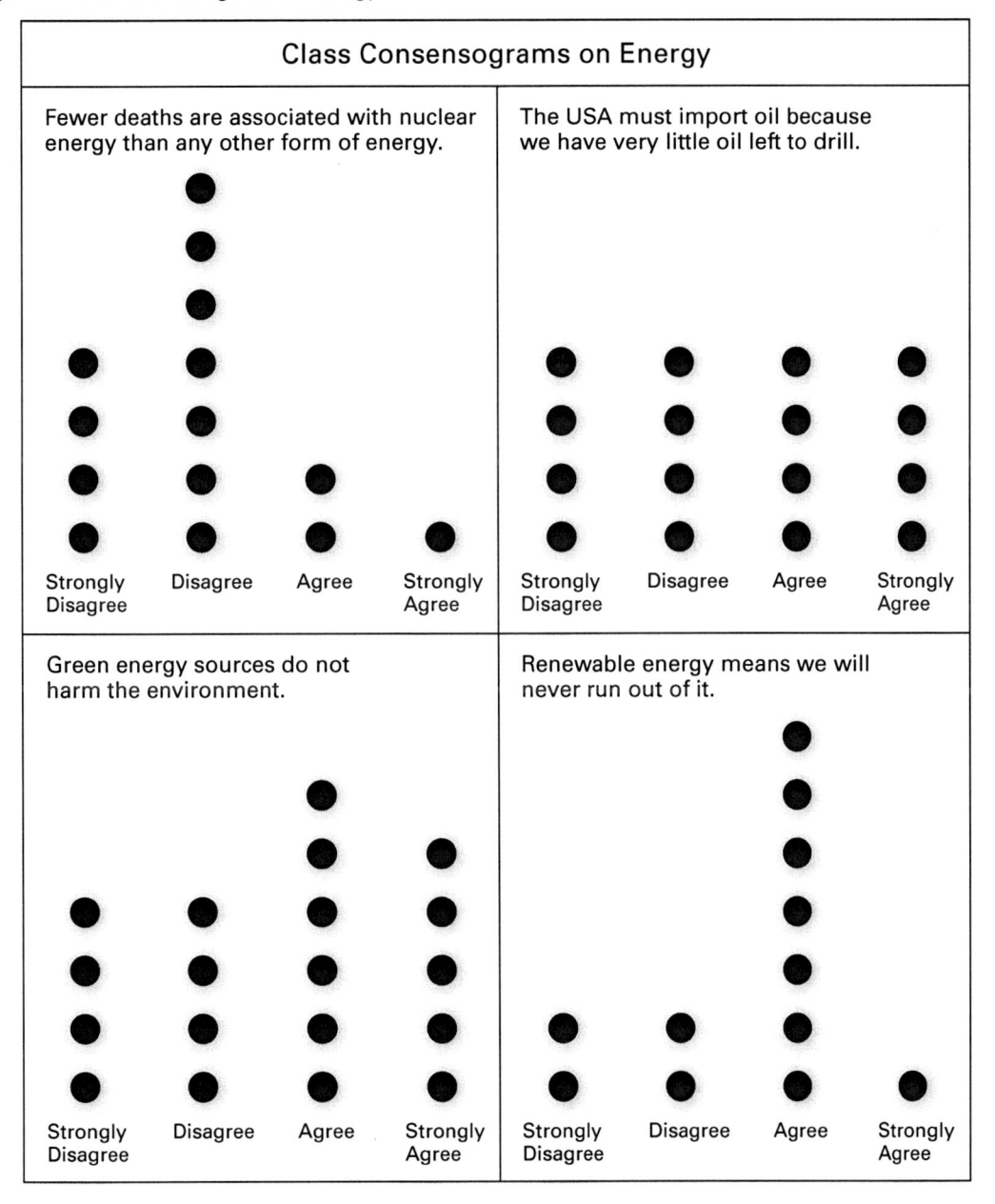

Class Consensograms on Energy

Fewer deaths are associated with nuclear energy than any other form of energy.

Strongly Disagree	Disagree	Agree	Strongly Agree
4	7	2	1

The USA must import oil because we have very little oil left to drill.

Strongly Disagree	Disagree	Agree	Strongly Agree
4	4	4	4

Green energy sources do not harm the environment.

Strongly Disagree	Disagree	Agree	Strongly Agree
4	4	5	4

Renewable energy means we will never run out of it.

Strongly Disagree	Disagree	Agree	Strongly Agree
2	2	7	1

Anticipatory Guide

Math: His class will study a geometry unit next, and Mr. Madaki is very curious about his students' levels of word recognition. He's not sure how much vocabulary students retain from their fourth grade study of geometry. Because his students love their new iPads, he is going to use a free online survey tool (see Appendix) as an anticipatory guide. The digital tool will automatically engage some students, and a real benefit is that he and the class will get instant feedback on the level of vocabulary mastery. At the end of the unit, he can use this same tool to track growth. He creates a series of questions similar to this one.

Figure 1.3 Online survey question example

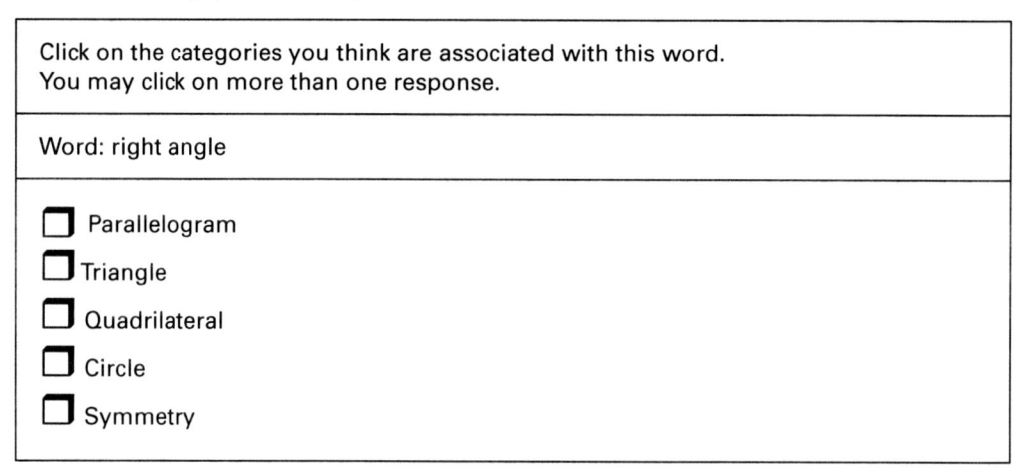

Click on the categories you think are associated with this word. You may click on more than one response.
Word: right angle
☐ Parallelogram ☐ Triangle ☐ Quadrilateral ☐ Circle ☐ Symmetry

When everyone is done, he calls up the summary of results from the site that looks something like this:

Figure 1.4 Online survey summary of results

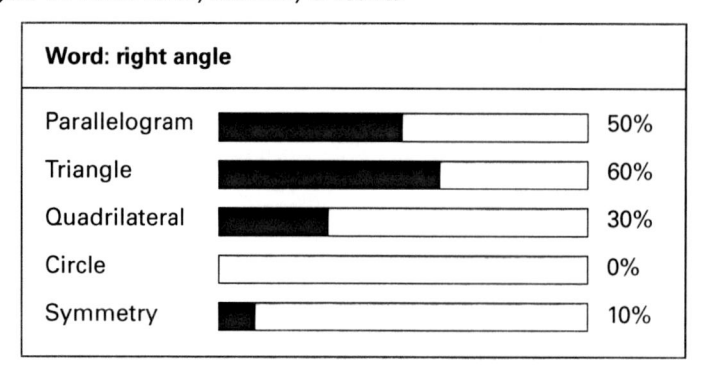

Word: right angle		
Parallelogram	▬▬▬▬▬▬	50%
Triangle	▬▬▬▬▬▬▬	60%
Quadrilateral	▬▬▬	30%
Circle		0%
Symmetry	▬	10%

He is relieved that no one associates right angles with circles. However, it is clear that a large percentage of students have not internalized the relationship between 90° angles and parallelograms, quadrilaterals, and triangles. Looking at the results of all the key questions, he identifies misconceptions, gaps in knowledge, and concepts students have already mastered. He holds a data discussion similar to the science teacher's.

- What do you notice?
- What surprises you?
- Which words does it appear we know very well as a class?
- Which words do we really need to clarify as a class?
- What other information do we need to guarantee that people are clear about the definition of each of these words?
- Where outside of this class might it be important to understand these words?
- What are some strategies we might use to make sure everyone knows all of the words at the end of the unit?

Now Mr. Madaki has some specific data about what students remember from previous units and about which topics students are confused. He confirms that there are different levels of student mastery within the class and that a one-size-fits-all approach to the unit will not be appropriate. He still needs more specific data on individual students, so he will use formative assessments throughout the unit to track individual student progress. Also, he has hooked the students by involving them in using their own data as a basis for upcoming lessons, in generating ideas for learning strategies, and by suggesting there are reasons beyond the classroom for knowing this vocabulary. Finally, Mr. Madaki is modeling a discussion that focuses on digging into data by identifying what other information is needed. Hopefully, students' awareness is raised about the importance of rationally exploring results of an inquiry rather than jumping to conclusions without considering the quality or quantity of the data.

Benefits

The anticipatory guide is a flexible strategy that can be adapted for use with individuals, small groups, or the entire class. It might be a paper-and-pencil activity, one that involves charts and student movement, or one done entirely on the computer or with a clicker system. Because the teacher can immediately recognize the level of student background knowledge regarding a topic, he or she can refine the instructional plan to address gaps, misconceptions, and advanced knowledge. Engaged by the well-written, intriguing guide statements, students discuss the major concepts and big ideas in the upcoming unit. These discussions and resulting charts help less confident students distinguish between the important and not-so-important ideas in upcoming readings. Because the anticipatory guide works well in a paper-and-pencil classroom and can be altered to appeal to digital natives, it remains a viable and effective instructional tool.

At the Mall

Description

A cooperative learning activity that incorporates movement and chatting with classmates is the basis for this strategy. Students enjoy the chance to get up out of their seats and talk with friends from across the room even though the process is very structured.

The strategy begins with students placed in small "home" groups of four or five. The purpose of these groups is twofold: to gather information about the new topic to be studied and to formulate questions that will be used to help focus student learning. While in their home group, each student receives a piece of information or data related to what is about to be studied.

They leave their home group and stroll the imaginary "mall" of their classroom. Providing some mall-type decorations can add some fun and novelty to the activity. At a signal, students stop and chat with another mall crawler who is not in their home group. Each student must work into the conversation the information or data they were given. Again, at a signal, they stroll around and stop when instructed, talking with another student and sharing information. The process continues for a few minutes, and then all students return to their home groups.

Back in their home groups, they share and record what new information they remember. At the very least, they have their own data points to share, and most will remember at least one other new piece of information. The groups review the information they have gathered, and then formulate questions based upon it. These questions will be answered as the lesson or unit proceeds. What's important is that they are the students' questions rather than the teachers'—that bit of student ownership builds enthusiasm.

Purpose

- Build interest in the upcoming topic and elicit student questions
- Begin building vocabulary
- Provide an opportunity for students to interact and work with a variety of students in their class

How It Differentiates

- Provides movement for students who have trouble sitting still for lengthy periods of time
- Allows students who prefer thinking out loud to process ideas orally
- Provides experience and training for collaborative group work
- Supplies less able readers with key words and clues about the big ideas

Procedure for Teacher

1. Review the text or video students will be using and develop a list of key phrases. The list should contain one phrase for each student in the class. For example, if the class were going to read an article on chromosomes, phrases might include:

    - Chromosomes are found in cells.
    - Chromosomes are threadlike material.
    - Most of us have 23 pairs of chromosomes.
    - Our genes hang out in our chromosomes.

2. Write each phrase on a separate index card.
3. Divide the class up into groups of 3–5 students. This will be their home group.
4. Hand an index card to each student. Explain that the classroom has become their favorite mall and help students imagine the scene by pointing out landmarks—the white board is McDonalds, where they might stop for a snack; the back bulletin board is the video game gallery. Be playful! Explain that they will wander the mall until they hear you say "STOP!"
5. Each student then finds a partner nearby, reads his or her card to the partner, and listens as the partner reads his or her own card.

6. Then they start the mall crawl again until they hear STOP, and they read their cards again. Variations are: (1) they can trade cards, or (2) some cards may have images, and students discuss what they see.

7. Go through 5 or 6 rotations, and then have students return to their home groups. Play popular music as students move about the room.

8. In their home groups, instruct them to list everything they remember on a sheet of paper.

9. Each home group shares their list, and the lists are recorded on a big chart or in a class wiki that an LCD projector is displaying from a computer screen. It is important that everyone is able to see the chart because it will have key ideas, characteristics, people, places, and events associated with the next topic of study. Students begin to build their mental maps of the topic with ideas and new vocabulary.

10. Each home group reviews the information, and based on that information, they generate some questions. If students are not used to formulating questions, the teacher will need to model the process through a Think Aloud (see Appendix).

11. Post the questions and refer to them during the lesson or unit as they are answered.

12. As you make the class chart or wiki list, start a word wall for the unit. Have students identify key words from the chart and put them on chart paper, in a wiki, or if you are in a 1 to 1 digital device classroom, students can write them on a Stickie Note (a free download). Use the word wall throughout the unit to review the specific vocabulary associated with the content studied (see Appendix).

Content Examples

Health: Mrs. Holmes' class will next study the relationship between diet and health. She plans to use several Internet resources for text-based discussions. Facts such as these from http://www.vivavegie.org/101book/text/nolink/social/supersizeme.html provide the content for an At the Mall activity:

- In the U.S., we eat more than 1,000,000 animals an hour.
- 60 percent of all Americans are either overweight or obese.
- One in every three children born in the year 2000 will develop diabetes in their lifetime.
- Having diabetes can cut 17–27 years off your life.

Mrs. Holmes explains the activity and its purpose to her students and then has them organize into their home groups. She hands out the note cards to each student and turns on some Justin Beiber music. Naturally some students groan about her selection, so she promises to play hip hop music for the next round as she sends them off to circulate and share sound bites of information. After trading factoids, the students return to their home groups and make their lists. When the groups share with the entire class, a lengthy class chart develops.

Home groups then huddle again and generate questions such as *What is diabetes? Why does diabetes affect how long you will live?* The teacher has (1) piqued students' interest, (2) introduced some key vocabulary, and (3) created a bank of student-generated questions she can use to shape upcoming lessons. The teacher has differentiated by providing movement that many boys need and an opportunity to collaborate which appeals to many females. Students have opportunities to socialize, verbalize, and see ideas analyzed and categorized on charts. A thirty-minute student-centered learning activity has quickly focused the students' attention on the big ideas of the upcoming nutrition unit.

Language Arts: The class is going to read O'Henry's short story "The Ransom of Red Chief." Knowing that the setting of the story and vocabulary may be difficult for some students to relate to, Mr. Kasawski carefully chooses short quotes from the story to begin building prior knowledge.

- "There was a town down there, as flat as a flannel-cake, and called Summit, of course."
- "We're making Buffalo Bill's show look like magic-lantern views of Palestine in the town hall."
- "He immediately christened me Snake-eye, the Spy, and announced that, when his braves returned from the warpath, I was to be broiled at the stake at the rising of the sun."
- "'I don't have any fun at home.' 'I hate to go to school.' 'I like to camp out.'"
- "Over toward Summit I expected to see the sturdy yeomanry of the village armed with scythes and pitchforks beating the countryside for the dastardly kidnappers."

Figure 2.1 Example of a Home Group Chart

Home Group Chart					
Setting	Characters	Plot	Conflict	Point of View	Theme
Summit—it's flat In the past—time of Buffalo Bill	Sam Driscoll A boy Person telling the story	Kidnapping The boy is driving the kidnappers crazy.	Boy and kidnappers Boy doesn't like his life.	Told from the point of view of kidnappers	Be careful what you wish for

He arranges the students into heterogeneous home groups and proceeds with the next steps of the activity. After several rotations, the students return to their home groups and share what they remember from the quotes they heard. Recording their information digitally in the class wiki, they identify words they don't know that prevent them from understanding the text. Using Google forms, available on the Google Docs site, Mr. Kawaski has created a chart (see Figure 2.1) that lists short story elements. Home groups collaborate on filling in these charts with information they have gathered.

Students use the clues in the quotes to predict what will happen, which is a key reading skill. This chart acts as a type of advance organizer for students when they begin to read or listen to the short story independently. Also, choosing quotes that only hint at the action rather than give away the plot intrigues students to read and find out what really happens in the story.

Mr. Kawaski is thinking about extending this activity by asking students to connect what they so far know of O'Henry's characters to contemporary characters from fiction, TV, or the movies. Linking the rascally, kidnapped lad to bad boy characters should be relatively easy for his students and will provide additional connections for those who need support in understanding the relationships in the short story.

Furthermore, this activity gives him an opportunity to help students picture a setting that is much different from any they have experienced. He might even ask a couple volunteers to sketch on the board the setting as they imagine it. O'Henry and many other authors present students with challenging vocabulary that may also be outside their experience. Having students identify words that keep them from understanding what is happening will provide Mr. K much fodder for great vocabulary lessons. Because the breadth of a student's vocabulary is a great predictor of future academic success, he knows the minutes spent on this activity are well worth class time.

Art: Ms. Kachur decides to adapt this activity to the digital age by using a wiki; instead of going to the mall, students will visit a virtual museum she created on the class wiki. The wiki has multiple pages, each with a unique image representing some aspect of the upcoming photography unit. Page one has an Ansel Adams image; the next page features a Margaret Bourke-White image; page three shows an example of a student's work; and so on.

Students pair up and comment on their observations of each image. Ms. Kachur offers guidance on focusing their comments—subject, color, perspective, use of light and dark, etc. Below is a sample wiki page. Notice that each student's name and a time stamp is provided, so Mrs. K. knows which comment belongs to whom and when it was added to the wiki. Students are also able to read each others' comments.

Figure 2.2 Sample wiki page

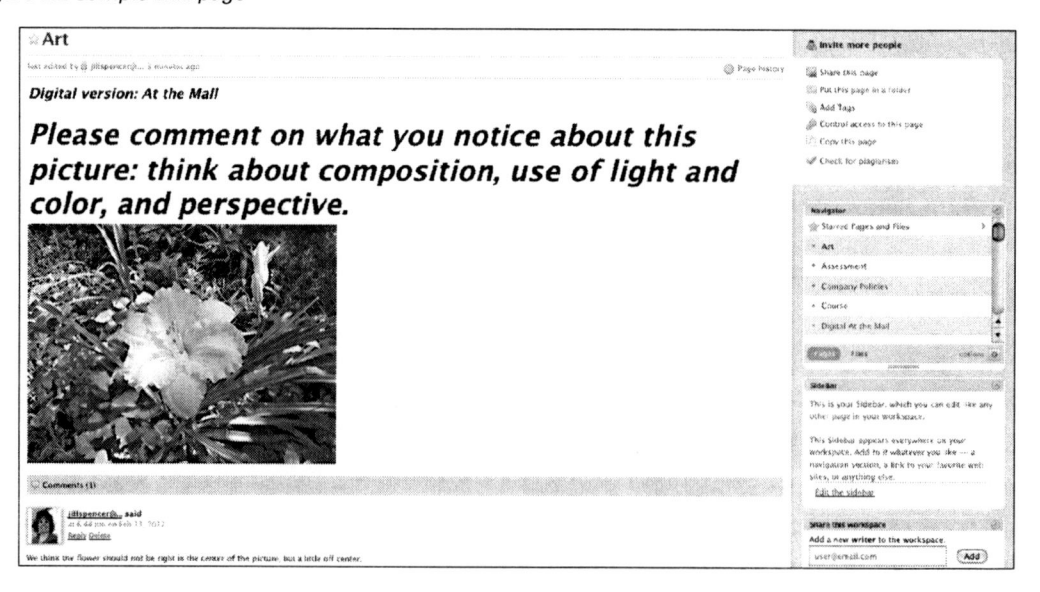

When all of the partners have viewed and commented on the images, partners are paired so there are groups of four. Groups review all of the comments and make a list of criteria of what makes a stunning picture. Several students have reading or visual impairments, so they use digital text-to-speech applications to help them successfully complete the task. (Apple products have text-to-speech capability built in, and there are free downloads for PCs.) That list of criteria is a great lead into specific lessons on how to recognize and shoot spectacular photographs. While assessing what students remember about art concepts such as composition from previous units, Ms. Kachur is also differentiating by addressing a variety of learning preferences and needs.

Benefits

At the Mall is a change-of-pace activity that takes advantage of young adolescents' love of socializing and provides a motor break for those who need to move to better refocus. It is also a way to introduce critical vocabulary in context to those students with limited academic background knowledge. Repetitive recitation of the short excerpts will help students needing practice with their reading fluency. Potentially, the home groups afford the teacher an opportunity to cluster students in a variety of ways—heterogeneously or putting advanced students together or creating single gender groups—depending on the needs of each individual class. Students see, hear, and synthesize information from several sources and then generate their own questions to help them focus on the upcoming lessons. Taking students to the mall where they love to hang out, even if it is just in their imaginations, will get them up and engaged in talking about the upcoming topic.

Expanded KWL
Using an Article or Film Clip

Description

KWL stands for What I Already **Know**, What I **Want** to Learn, What I **Learned**. Often used before students read a selection or start a new unit, this activity is designed to access prior knowledge, generate questions, and then summarize new learning. When using this strategy, teachers can become frustrated by student reactions such as *I don't know anything about this topic, and I don't want to learn anything about it.* Such a response results in a disappointing start for the lesson or unit and teachers' reluctance to use KWL again. Students' reactions are justified if they have very little background knowledge to call upon during a KWL exercise, which makes it difficult to engage in the lesson. Providing students with some intriguing background information from an article or video will engage their natural curiosity and make the activity a success.

By introducing background information to the class, everyone in the class is able to contribute ideas for the KWL chart, not just students with a lot of general academic background knowledge. The choice of the article or video to use is important: it should be interesting as well as related to the unit content, and contain some specific information that will engage more advanced students. Taking time to stop one or two times during the video or the reading will allow students the opportunity to talk about the content. Thus, the social learners get to talk about the ideas, and struggling students will hear points clarified during the course of reading the article or watching the video, which will help them as they progress through the lesson.

Purpose

- Build interest and elicit student questions
- Introduce new vocabulary
- Introduce background knowledge students need to understand new information
- Identify prior knowledge and uncover misconceptions

How It Differentiates

- Provides the opportunity to assign articles of differing reading levels and complexity
- Allows students who prefer thinking out loud to process ideas
- Provides opportunities for learning collaborative and cooperative skills
- Provides for students who like to work in groups
- Provides vocabulary, images, and information to support students lacking specific background knowledge needed for understanding the new topic.

Procedure for Teacher:

1. Using paper or a wiki, create a template such as the one below that students can follow as they work through the activity.

Expanded KWL Chart			
What We **KNOW** from the article/video clip	What We **KNOW** from our own background knowledge	What We **Want** to Find Out	What We **Learned**

2. Choose a high-interest article related to your topic. Print copies, turn it into a transparency, or show it on a screen with an LCD projector (see Appendix).

3. Group students in pairs.

4. Review the KWL strategy with your students. Explain that they will work in pairs to fill in the first two columns of their individual sheets. Also, have a chart ready to record ideas from the class.

5. Spend time with the students reading the article or watching the clip, and discuss the content. You might do a Think Aloud as you read the article out loud or stop the video in appropriate spots.

    - Read aloud the beginning of the text, and then think out loud. Describe how you are processing the text. Read a bit more and continue your thinking out loud.
    - Read aloud another chunk of text and invite students to participate.
    - Continue until you have finished the piece.
    - When using video clips, stop the video at an intriguing spot and do the Think Aloud. Stop again and invite students to join in.
    - Some schools block YouTube and other video sites. A way around those restrictions is to use Zamzar.com. This free site will convert Internet video into a .mov format and e-mail you a link, so you can download the video to your laptop at home. Bring it to school on a thumb drive and load it onto your school computer.

6. Next, have partners fill in the left column using information from the shared article/video and any background information they possess.

7. Refocus the entire class on a chart or LCD screen and fill in the left-hand column together on the class chart.

8. Then ask partners to discuss column #2 with each other. Once again, bring everyone's attention back to the class chart, and fill the column with ideas from the class.

9. Ask groups to review their information and generate some questions. If students are not used to generating questions, you will need to model the process of looking at text and asking questions. These questions go in column #3.

Students now have pertinent background information and perhaps some images to connect to their new information. Generating the questions will help students who have trouble with reading comprehension identify big, important ideas to pay special attention to as they read. Because the questions are student-generated, good readers will also be identifying questions that interest them. Finally, the chart serves as a visual scaffold to help everyone focus on the upcoming lessons and tasks.

The process of referring to the student-generated questions as the lesson or unit progresses helps students stay focused on key learnings. At the end of the unit, return to the chart and have students summarize the unit's big ideas. As a keen observer of this part of the process, you will be able to identify whether the goals have been met or whether students need some reteaching.

Content Examples

Science: An astronomy unit is in progress, and the upcoming lessons focus on space exploration. Ms. Grant grabs the students' attention by playing the beginning of Orson Welles' original *War of the Worlds* broadcast (http://www.archive.org/details/OrsonWellesMrBruns). The novelty of listening to an old radio show that is about an invasion of Earth by Martians holds the students' attention for a bit. They are a visual generation, and talk soon turns to the Spielberg movie which most of them have seen. Seizing upon the students' interest, Ms. Grant asks them to pair up and look at the KWL chart. She asks them to fill in what they know for sure about Mars and space exploration (column 2).

Figure 3.1 KWL Chart on Mars and Space Exploration

KWL Chart on Mars and Space Exploration			
What We **KNOW** from the image and caption	What We **KNOW** from our own background knowledge	What We **Want** to Find Out	What We **Learned**
	• Mars looks red from Earth. • Writers have used it as a setting in science fiction. • It's one of the closest planets to us. • There is an international space station. • We've sent rockets out into space to explore.		

After students share, she puts up a picture from the Astronomy Picture of the Day site entitled "Seasonal Dark Streaks on Mars" (August 8, 2011). The image of these dark streaks on Mars is accompanied by the following text (http://apod.nasa.gov/apod/astropix.html):

> **Explanation:** What is causing these dark streaks on Mars? A leading hypothesis is flowing—but quickly evaporating—water. The streaks, visible in dark brown near the image center, appear in the Martian spring and summer but fade in the winter months, only to reappear again the next summer. These are not the first markings on Mars that have been interpreted as showing the effects of running water, but they are the first to add the clue of a seasonal dependence. The above picture, taken in May, digitally combines several images from the HiRISE instrument on the Mars Reconnaissance Orbiter (MRO). The image is color-enhanced and depicts a slope inside Newton crater in a mid-southern region of Mars. The streaks bolster evidence that water exists just below the Martian surface in several locations, and therefore fuels speculation

Expanded KWL 47

that Mars might harbor some sort of water-dependent life. Future observations with robotic spacecraft orbiting Mars, such as MRO, Mars Express, and Mars Odyssey will continue to monitor the situation and possibly confirm—or refute—the exciting flowing water hypothesis.

She does a Think Aloud, stopping after every couple of sentences to ask the students what they can add to column number 1.

Figure 3.2 KWL Chart on Mars and Space Exploration

KWL Chart on Mars and Space Exploration			
What We **KNOW** from the image and caption	What We **KNOW** from our own background knowledge	What We **Want** to Find Out	What We **Learned**
• Some think there has been flowing water on Mars- brown streaks. • Streaks disappear in winter months. • There is a Mars Reconnaissance Orbiter.	• Mars looks red from Earth. • Writers have used it as a setting in science fiction. • It's one of the closest planets to us. • There is an international space station. • We've sent rockets out into space to explore.		

After the students wring every bit of information out of the image and caption and list it in column #1, Ms. Grant asks them to review the two columns and to formulate some driving questions for the next part of the unit. Great questions emerge:

- Why do we bother to explore space—how does it help us here on earth?
- What does a planet need to be like in order for it to have life?

- How do scientists figure out how to build and guide a rocket to a specific part of space?
- What sorts of things are astronomers learning besides there might be water on Mars?

She is pleased with the questions. They align very well with the standard she wants her students to meet. ***Students will gain knowledge about the universe and how humans have learned about it, and about the principles upon which it operates. Students will be able to:*** *Describe scientists' exploration of space and the objects they have found (Maine State Learning Results).* Furthermore, the process has allowed her do a little coaching on the wording of the questions so that more critical thinking will occur.

By using images, text, a Think Aloud, and collaborative effort within the KWL strategy, Ms. Grant is sure that each student has enough prior knowledge to successfully proceed with the next section of the lesson.

French: The class is slated to read a description of Paris. Monsieur LeBlanc wants them to develop an appreciation of the city of Paris and its beautiful architecture and gardens. Because many students have not traveled extensively and may not have mental images of monumental arches, cathedrals, sculptures, boulevards, and formal gardens, he helps them create mental pictures of the things they will be reading about by using the expanded KWL chart coupled with a Google Earth tour of Paris. First, he assesses their background information by asking them what they know about Paris. As they share, he fills in the second column of the expanded KWL chart—What do we know for sure about Paris?

Then he opens up Google Earth (see Appendix) and focuses on their hometown. The satellite view of their town comes into view and the students can easily pick out their school. Then, he types "Paris, France" and hits "return." The image of the town rapidly goes into motion and fades back to a wide angle view of their part of the country. The Mississippi River and the Great Lakes come into view. The students track the satellite image as it continues to spin further away from their town and travels across half of the United States, the Atlantic Ocean, and zeroes in on Paris. Once there, he highlights many of the most famous Paris sites, and their pictures and French names pop up: l'Arc de Triomphe, Jardin du Luxembourg, etc. Then the class walks at street level down the Paris boulevards. In column number 1 of their KWL charts, students do a quick sketch of the places they have seen via Google Earth in Paris and label them appropriately in French. Now, when they read, they will have a visual to accompany the vocabulary word. The final step before students read independently is to have them generate questions about Paris that they want to find answers for as they read.

While the class was visiting Paris via Google Earth, Mr. Connelly had poked his head in the door to deliver a message. Observing the students' engagement in the upcoming lesson, he immediately thought, "Hmmm, I wonder if Google Earth has the battlefields of the Civil War?" He went back to his room and located the Gettysburg Battlefield—there was Cemetery Ridge, Lee's location, and the starting point of Pickett's Charge. He began to revise his upcoming lesson.

Advisory: All of the advisory groups were beginning to explore the multi-faceted topic of cyber citizenship. The first part of the unit focused on teen use of the Internet. To ensure that students were working from fact rather than perception, the advisors shared statistics from the Pew Research Center's Internet and American Life Project Trend Data for Teens:

Data Trends for Teenage Use of Internet	
Online Activities	**% of teen Internet users in the U.S. as of September 2009**
Use social networking like My Space or Facebook	73
Get news or information about politics or current events	62
Buy things	48
Share something they have created	38
Use Twitter	8
Visit virtual worlds	8

Source: http://www.pewinternet.org/Static-Pages/Trend-Data-for-Teens/Online-Activites-Total.aspx

As students were filling in information in column 1 of their individual KWL charts—What Do We KNOW about teen use of the Internet from the Pew Research Project?—they started to grumble quite vociferously. "This can't be right—everyone uses Twitter." The wily advisors, of course, had set up the scenario hoping for an opportunity for some critical thinking and questioning of published data.

"What do you notice about the data?" they queried.
"It's wrong."
"It's stupid!"
And finally, "It's out of date!"
The advisors agreed and quickly changed the headings of the KWL chart to:

Figure 3.3 Expanded KWL Chart on Teenage Use of the Internet

Expanded KWL Chart on Teenage Use of the Internet			
What We **KNOW** about teen use of the Internet in 2009	What We **THINK WE KNOW** about teen use of the Internet in 2011	What We **Want** to Find Out	What We **Learned**

The next step was of course to generate questions that would lead to accurate statistics. Students were instantly engaged to prove the statistics wrong and out-of-date. In the process, they would uncover a factual overview of current teen use of the Internet, which would be perfect for future discussions on the pluses and minuses of Internet use, a self-reflection on their own use of the Internet, and perhaps a prediction of what will come next in the digital age.

Benefits

By using the enhanced KWL strategy, teachers access, assess, and build students' prior knowledge. There is individual think time for the internal processors and time to share ideas for the external processors. According to Gurian and Stevens (2011), proponents of gender differences in learning, in general, girls find it easier than boys to integrate cooperative learning skills into their learning process (p. 93). So most girls will be very comfortable with the collaborative aspects of this strategy, and as collaboration is considered a critical 21st century skill, everyone will benefit from the opportunity to work together. Images are also part of the strategy, which helps those who lack background knowledge and those who need concrete examples to internalize new learning. With the use of a chart and discussion, any students with auditory or visual impairments are able to access the information. Finally, students who struggle with identifying what is and what is not important while reading or viewing can use the generated questions to help them take notes in the upcoming lessons. Also, the questions generated, with coaching from the teacher, will span Bloom's taxonomy and spur the most advanced students to dig deeper into the topic.

Carousel

Description

Picture a merry-go-round with the riders traveling in circles. In the carousel activity students circle the classroom in small groups responding to prompts written on chart paper posted at various points. This strategy not only allows the teacher to identify strengths and gaps in students' knowledge base in a non-threatening way, but it also reviews and brings to the forefront important unit or lesson vocabulary. Discussing each prompt they encounter, the students travel around the carousel in groups of 3 to 5. Because the responses are a group effort, the "spotlight" is never on an individual student, and students do not worry about being singled out for an answer. Adolescent boys, especially, will do anything not to appear stupid or silly in front of their peers, so working with a group allows them to add useful information when they know it and just to listen when they don't. The carousel is also helpful for students with expressive language issues who have trouble retrieving information or spelling words correctly. The charts scaffold the learning by providing prompts that help students demonstrate what they already know. The physical movement also addresses the need for students who find it difficult to remain still for long periods of time. Encouraging students to use images as well as words helps out the visual learner. This activity can also be adapted for use on computers making it engaging for digital learners. The carousel activity is a simple but multi-faceted way to differentiate.

Purpose

- Build interest and elicit student questions
- Ascertain level of student prior knowledge
- Identify any existing misperceptions

How It Differentiates

- Adds movement to the class structure
- Provides a visual prompt for those who need to see words or concepts written to understand them
- Gives students who need to talk through ideas orally a chance to process
- Builds vocabulary and background information
- Allows for advanced students to be grouped together to share and discuss ideas
- Uses words and phrases, which eases the stress for students who have difficulty reading lengthy text
- Allows students with expressive language issues an opportunity to add to what others have already stated
- Provides an opportunity for ELL students both to see and hear new vocabulary

Procedure

1. Identify what prior knowledge students need to be successful in the upcoming lesson or unit.
2. Craft 4-6 open-ended prompts that will elicit from students what they think they know about the topic. Write these prompts on individual charts or pages of a wiki (see Appendix). Prompts may be:
   - Text.
   - Images.
   - Audio or video.
3. Decide how you will display the prompts:
   - Individual chart paper
   - Wiki or Google docs
4. Divide students into groups of 3 or 4.
5. Station each group at a different chart or assign them a wiki page and have them:
   - Read the prompt.
   - Talk among themselves about possible responses to the prompt.
   - Record their best thinking.

6. After a set time (2 or 3 minutes), have students move to the next prompt.
7. Instruct students to read both the prompt and responses and then add to the responses.
8. Repeat the rotations. It's great when students can respond to all of the prompts; however, the time available will dictate the number of group moves.
9. Bring the class together to review the charts.
10. Make notes on any incorrect information that you will need to address during the unit. If each group is given a different color marker, and they use it for the entire process, teachers can keep track of who is responsible for the responses. This information will be helpful for forming future groups and meeting with students who need some sort of intervention before the unit begins.
11. Use charts as a vehicle for discussion to
    - Generate questions.
    - Write summaries.
    - Make predictions.

Content Examples

Industrial Arts/Technology: Every year the Rube Goldberg Contraption Unit (http://www.rubegoldberg.com/ and http://sciencespot.net/Pages/spmachinfo.html) is a favorite with both teachers and students.

Figure 4.1 Students at Mt. Ararat Middle School in Topsham, Maine, incorporated a pulley, a lever, and a screw to create this Rube Goldberg contraption.

Using their understanding of the six simple machines (pulleys, levers, wedges, wheels and axles, incline planes, and screws), students build contraptions that actually complete a task. Mr. Strong and Mrs. Ford know that their students studied simple machines the previous year in science, but they don't know which concepts they may need to reteach and which ones just need a review before the unit begins.

The teachers decide to use a carousel activity to assess students' prior knowledge. This approach will give them an overview of the class's knowledge. They simply make six posters, one for each of the simple machines.

Figure 4.2 Simple Machine Charts

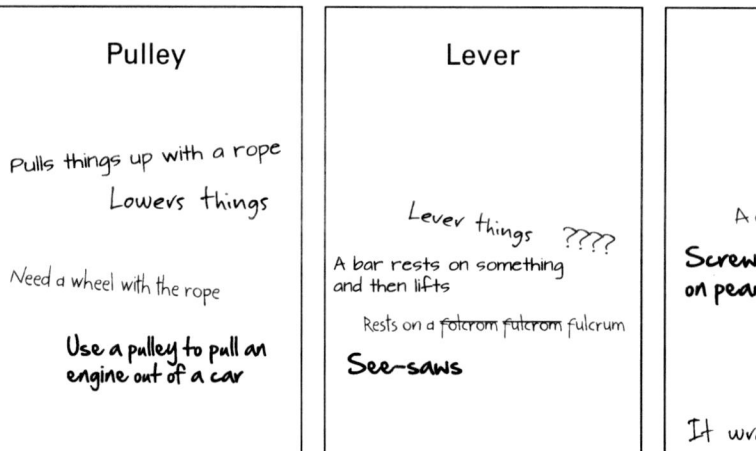

Pulley	Lever	Screw
Pulls things up with a rope Lowers things Need a wheel with the rope Use a pulley to pull an engine out of a car	Lever things ???? A bar rests on something and then lifts Rests on a folcrom fulcrom fulcrum See-saws	A drill is a kind of screw Screw on jar cap like on peanut butter Some how it's like an incline plane??? It wraps around

They organize students into groups of three. Each group uses a different color marker, so the teacher can track which groups are responsible for which comments. The groups each start at a different chart. The teacher delivers a very simple prompt: "Using words and images, record what you know about the simple machine listed at the top of the chart." The groups stay at the first chart for about 2 minutes, and then they move on. The time at each chart decreases a bit because information is accumulating on the chart. If students see something on a chart that they think might be incorrect, they put a question mark next to it.

When the class has finished rotating through the charts, the teachers bring all the charts to the front and review them with the class. This review also addresses the question marks on the charts. Mrs. Ford notices that the group with the red marker in her period 3 class often recorded incorrect information. She will check her notes to see which students are in that group and plan a time when she can check in with them individually. Overall, the students remember a lot about most of the machines, however, the wedge has the least amount of information. Mrs. Ford decides she needs to reteach that concept before starting the unit.

Math: At the beginning of the year, Mr. Freeman wants to find out how at ease his students are with solving problems multiple ways. The seventh grade math classes meet in a tiny, odd-shaped room with eight tables of four students each. Because moving the students from chart to chart is very difficult in the confined space of his classroom, Mr. Freeman moves the charts from table to table.

He writes different problems at the top of each chart with the prompt "Solve this problem." Each table gets a chart and discusses an approach. They record their work, and then at the signal, pass the chart to the next table. The second round instruction asks the students to demonstrate an alternative way to solve the problem. The rotations continue as long as students are able to generate another procedure for problem solving. Mr. Freeman is edging his way around the tables listening closely to student discussions and making notes about their mathematical reasoning. He pays special attention to table number three. He has grouped there the students with the highest standardized test scores. He is curious to see if they think critically about math concepts, or if they are just really good at plugging numbers into memorized algorithms.

To end the prior knowledge segment of his lesson, Mr. Freeman shares the charts with the class. He asks them to reflect on what they see by asking questions like…

- What do you notice?
- What are some similarities among the charts?
- What are some differences?
- Which problem-solving strategies are the most efficient?
- Which problem-solving strategies work best for you? Why?

He wants students at all levels of mathematical sophistication to think about the processes they use in their work. The open-ended, metacognitive questions help each student think about their own learning. He has also been able to identify which students rely on "guess and check" a lot and makes a note to help them become better at identifying patterns. Because of the structure of this strategy, students of all abilities and learning strengths work together to reinforce what they already know and receive a bit of a review of those procedures they have not quite mastered.

Language Arts/Science: The language arts and science teachers are excited to collaborate on a unit focusing on energy needs in the 21st century. Mr. Diaz is delighted to have an opportunity to address the Common Core Standards as they relate to reading informational text, and Ms. Cuperin is looking for help in working on her state's science standard related to communicating effectively about scientific principles. Their school is also devoting a lot of professional training to literacy across the curriculum. Working together will be fun and productive.

Using the backward planning model, they have identified their outcomes and a final assessment. They are ready to move on to developing their building and assessing prior knowledge activity. The purposes for this activity include:

- Introducing new vocabulary.
- Finding out whether students understand the vocabulary they assume the students know.
- Identifying what the students already know about energy resources.
- Building student interest in the unit.

They decide to use a digital carousel activity for several reasons. This year's team has

- A visually impaired student who benefits from large print and hearing ideas discussed.
- Many students who are still developing their collaborative skills, so short cooperative activities help them practice listening to others and offering ideas in a group setting.
- Lots of students who explore the digital world outside of school and often grow impatient with traditional textbooks.
- Three ELL students who benefit from both seeing and hearing words and phrases associated with content.
- Several students who have difficulty expressing themselves in writing but are able to successfully join a discussion if someone else is the recorder.

Mr. Diaz already has a class wiki (see Appendix) set up and all of the students are registered at this site. They create a separate page for each prompt on the wiki to easily structure and supervise the activity. After discussion they decide on prompts including:

- What words do you associate with the use of energy in this country? (The teachers are curious if words such as renewable, solar, and wind power will show up.)
- What are some things you know about petroleum products? (They assume students know the word petroleum but are not sure.)
- What are examples of renewable energy? (The teachers are checking for prior knowledge.)
- Where do we get electricity? List as many sources as you can think of. (The teachers are checking for prior knowledge.)
- Click on this YouTube link and watch the video on renewable energy in which students show and describe their projects. What questions would you ask these students to find out more about hydrogen fuel cells and solar ovens? (Mr. Diaz and Ms. Cuperin think that seeing other students describe projects they built will pique their students' interest.)
- What are the benefits and drawbacks of nuclear energy? (The teachers are checking for prior knowledge.)
- Click on this link to read a short article on energy issues. Take a quick vote in your group on which issue presents the biggest challenge for the U.S. Write it on the chart with your justification. (The teachers want students thinking about the critical issues in energy production, and they will also see some new vocabulary used in context.)

Ms. Cuperin volunteers to use her class time for this activity because she wants to learn more about using wikis in her classes. She knows that if there are any problems, Mr. Diaz is just across the hall and that she has a class full of mini-experts who have all used wikis before. She has signed out the cart of laptops and has arranged ten around the room. She has also set the font size to 18 (see Appendix) to accommodate the needs of the student with sight problems.

After dividing the class into pairs or triads, she directs them to their starting computer station open to its wiki page. Ms. Cuperin then explains the process and purpose of the activity. She asks them to note that each page has an active link on it. She explains that if they finish their response to the prompt before she has them move to the next station, they should click on the link. It will take them to a video to watch or game to play. Most of the sites have been produced by the big energy companies, and are helpful in building some background knowledge for the students to use when generating inquiry questions later. They will also provide the teachers with an opportunity to help students understand the importance of knowing the originator of a website when evaluating it for reliability or bias.

Figure 4.3 Wiki opening page

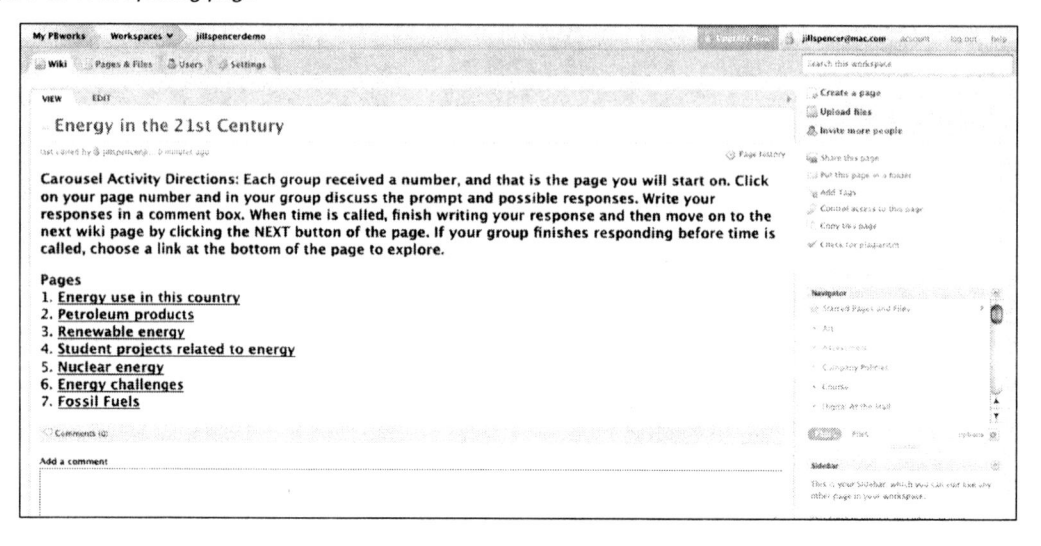

Figure 4.4 Wiki specific page

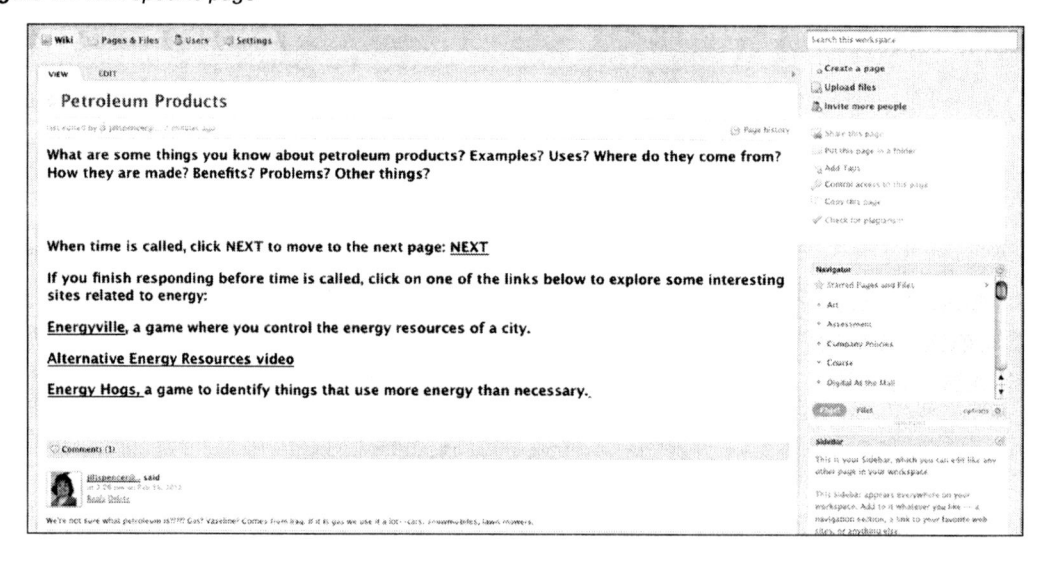

The lesson goes well as the students spend about five or six minutes at each station. Some ask if they can continue playing games like Energyville (http://www.energyville.com) later. After school Ms. Cuperin and Mr. Diaz review the wiki pages together. Glad they had decided not to assume the students understood what petroleum was, they found a lot of bad information on the wiki. Students also listed misinformation under the prompt on nuclear energy. Because students listed a lot of words associated with energy on the vocabulary prompt, they would spend time exploring with their students deeper understanding of these words. Especially pleased with the students' questions on several of the prompt pages, the teachers felt their objectives for the activity had been met and that they had good information to use in fine-tuning their plans for the upcoming unit. Noting misconceptions and other important information, they created several summary sheets on the wiki to use during the unit: Vocabulary We Need To Know; Things We're Curious About; and Information We Already Know! Mr. Diaz then deleted the wiki carousel pages; they did not want to leave any misinformation online.

Benefits

A carousel activity immediately appeals to students because they get to move around and talk with their peers. Beyond that, the structure of the carousel allows the teacher to engage students in higher-level thinking by crafting prompts that address different levels of Bloom's Taxonomy. Summarize, defend, support, compare, and justify—these verbs and others used in carousel prompts provide opportunities for all students to think beyond recall. Link well-written prompts with thoughtfully grouped students and the complexity of the conversations will vary depending on the cognitive development and the background knowledge of the participants. Another benefit is that ELL students and those with communication difficulties hear and see words and phrases used in context. Finally, the written record of the students' combined knowledge provides the teacher with specific evidence of the level of knowledge present and gives the students a big picture of where the lesson or unit is going to take them.

Children's Picture Books

Description

Children's picture books are wonderful teaching tools because the authors and illustrators take complex ideas and concepts and relay them with concise and engaging text and wonderful illustrations. Students are thus introduced to the concepts that they will be studying in a comfortable and non-threatening atmosphere. Most everyone, no matter their age, loves to hear children's literature read aloud. The group is transported back to kindergarten, and it becomes easier to ask questions without feeling like a dolt.

The colorful pictures also provide images students can use to connect to written ideas in their textbooks. Furthermore, many students, especially boys, do not have powerful vocabularies. The illustrations and clearly written text of the children's books gives them practice with both content-specific and academic vocabulary. By taking time to build students' background information, teachers will help their students be more successful at meeting the standards that form the basis of a unit.

Purpose

- Build interest and elicit student questions
- Begin to create mental maps of the concepts with images
- Begin to build vocabulary
- Introduce background knowledge students need to understand new information
- Allow students to practice their listening skills

How It Differentiates

- Provides an introduction of concepts and vocabulary in short sentences and paragraphs accompanied by detailed illustrations. This combination helps students with any type of language issue to see and hear ideas in a way that will not frustrate them.
- Builds common background knowledge for everyone and especially benefits children who have not had opportunities to travel, attend cultural events, or read extensively.
- Establishes a warm, nostalgic setting for students who are often ill at ease or unhappy in school.
- Sets up opportunities for both individual thinking time and small group discussion for introspective and interpersonal learners.

Procedure

There are several ways to use children's books to build prior knowledge and generate interest:

1. Choose one book to read aloud at the beginning of the unit. Read with gusto and stop along the way to invite students to participate:
    - Ask whether students know anything else about the topic or can give other examples.
    - Ask them to predict which words they are going to be responsible for and write them on the unit word wall.
    - Use a think-pair-share strategy to have students summarize important information.

2. Have several books on the topic available. Break the class up into small groups and hand them a book. Their job is to read the book together and report out on the big ideas. Chart the big ideas in a whole-class share; then follow up by asking students what other things they would like to know about the topic. An alternative to having students report out on the big ideas is to have each group create a skit that demonstrates the big ideas.

3. Use children's books that focus on the topic of the upcoming unit as sponge activities at the end of the class—the five minutes before the bell is going to ring. Read the books aloud. Start your word wall, ask students to add to what the text imparts, and share the illustrations. When the unit begins, students will have been

introduced to key vocabulary, seen images that will help them build mental maps, and heard basic concepts described. Some students may also like a chance to read aloud to their classmates.

4. Simply display the books in the room and invite students to read them when they have a few extra minutes. Have a graffiti board next to the display where students can post comments, ask questions, create drawings, etc. This graffiti board can be digital. A class wiki or digital bulletin board is easy to set up and monitor. Check out http://blog.corkboard.me/ to explore a free site that allows you to make a digital bulletin board for your class.

Not everyone has a vast knowledge of children's literature (see Appendix) to call upon. Local public and school librarians are resources to cultivate! They love to help people find books. Also, there are great resources on the web:

- Database of Award-Winning Children's Literature: http://dawcl.com/
- The Reading Nook: http://www.thereadingnook.com/
- Math in Children's Literature: http://ethemes.missouri.edu/themes/1154
- Math and Literature Idea Bank: http://www.mathcats.com/grownupcats/ideabankmathandliterature.html

Content Examples:

Language Arts: A new literature unit is beginning, and Mrs. Greenstone's sixth grade students must demonstrate that they understand the elements of the short story: setting, character, plot, conflict, point of view, and theme. She invites her students to go back in time to Read Alouds in kindergarten and gathers them around her as she reads them Leo Lionni's wonderful picture book *Swimmy* to introduce these concepts. Swimmy is a small fish whose family and friends are devoured by a monster-sized fish. Left alone, Swimmy sadly wanders the ocean waters. He slowly emerges from his funk as he experiences the wonders of the underwater world. Eventually, he finds some shy fish like himself and his leadership ability emerges! This beautifully illustrated story will allow Mrs. Greenstone to build the students' prior knowledge about the elements of the short story. As she reads, she stops periodically and asks students to pair up and respond to a question such as, "What does this action tell us about Swimmy?" At the end of the Read Aloud, the class discusses the story in terms of the six short story elements. As they read the stories in the unit, the concrete examples from *Swimmy* will provide a foundation for students' further learning.

Language Arts: Her seventh grade class is going to be reading *Lyddie*, award-winning author Katherine Paterson's novel of life in the textile mills from the point of view of one of the mill girls. Mrs. Greenstone's students live in suburbia more than a century later. They don't have a clue about textile mills or child labor in the United States. Mrs. Greenstone decides to build their prior knowledge through story and images. She reads aloud *The Bobbin Girl* by Emily Arnold McCully. In 30 pages full of illustrations, the story of Rebecca, a ten-year-old worker at the Lowell mills, unfolds. Images of the looming clock tower that regulates everyday life, descriptions of the stringent working conditions, and an account of the mill girls' battle with the powerful mill owners prepare the 21st century students for the themes and issues portrayed in *Lyddie*. An investment of 30-45 minutes of reading and discussion spread over several days ensures students will be able to connect the plot and characters of *Lyddie* to something they already know, a critical component of learning.

Mrs. Greenstone will extend this activity by having students research topics mentioned in the children's book that will help them understand and visualize the novel better:

- Build a model that shows how waterpower was turned into energy to run the looms.
- Create a chart that compares a mill worker's day with that of a modern teenager's.
- Create/draw a model of the Lowell Mill complex.
- Present an argument before the mill owners for a ten-hour work day limit.
- Research child labor in other parts of the world and connect it to the everyday products the students use regularly (e.g. soccer balls).

Finding entry points that engage the entire class in the reading of a single novel is hard work and an important aspect of building and accessing prior knowledge. Tapping into learning strengths, connecting issues to the students' current lives, and making unfamiliar settings familiar through images and experiences are effective differentiation strategies. Children's books help the teacher accomplish these goals.

Social Studies: "We're going to a station on the Underground Railroad—right here in town?" "I didn't know we had trains here." "Will we get to go underground into a big tunnel?" These enthusiastic questions alerted Ms. Farra that the students had many misconceptions about the Underground Railroad and its purpose. It became crystal clear that she needed to help students understand the 5Ws about the Underground Railroad before they went on the field trip the next week.

Knowing there were some very good children's books about the Underground Railroad, she enlisted the school librarian to ask the elementary school librarians to send the middle school any books that they had available. Ten arrived, and that meant she could break the class up into groups of three—each with a different book. Some of the books were easier than others, so she was mindful of reading ability as she grouped her students. Next, she had to build interest in the books; her students might not just dive into the reading. A Word Splash would do the trick!

In the days before Web 2.0 tools, Ms. Farra made Word Splashes by writing important words from the text in different colors and sizes all over an overhead transparency and flashed it up on the screen. The colors, different sizes, and the random arrangement of words grabbed students' attention. She would go through the children's books and pull out key words for the Word Splash: conductor, North Star, Canada, fugitive, Harriet Tubman, Underground Railroad, slaves, plantation, slave hunter, spirituals, railroad agent, dogs, secret compartments, freedom, Ohio River, quarters, master, hiding, overseer, whip.

Now, sometimes, she would make the Word Splashes digitally at Wordle.net, a site that transforms her word lists into a colorful word cloud (see Appendix). To prepare for class the next day, she created the Word Splash prompt with the key words as a word cloud at Wordle.net and uploaded the image to the wiki.

Figure 5.1 *Word Splash*

Children's Picture Books

She also decided to experiment with Twitter (see Appendix). She gave the class the name of a Twitter account she had set up just for her class and told the students to check it out that evening at 7 p.m. At 7 p.m. she tweeted, "What do these words have to do with the Underground Railroad: hiding, overseer, Ohio River, Tubman, conductor?" The tweet was less than 140 characters, so it went spinning out over the Internet. By 8 p.m., 25 of her students had tweeted a reply. Some of them, at least, were already thinking about possible word connections in the next day's activity! She copied the tweets into the class wiki, and planned on sharing them to start class the next day.

The next day class began by reviewing the tweets from the night before. Together as a class they starred the tweets they thought had accurate connections and put question marks next to the ones they thought might be less reliable. Next, the students paired up and used the words in the wiki chart in sentences that predicted what might happen in the library books they were going to read. Ms. Farra had the pairs star the sentences they thought were probably not true, and then she asked for volunteers to share some of them. Naturally, some of the sentences were pretty silly, so they got the giggling out of the way. Then she asked pairs to circle the sentences they thought were their best predictions and to post these sentences on the class wiki's Word Splash page. Using the comment feature of the wiki, everyone could post at the same time which eliminated taking turns to post.

Some of the sentences included:
- Slaves hid from the slave catchers in secret compartments.
- Slaves got whipped if they got caught running away to Canada.
- The Underground Railroad had conductors and agents, and it went north.

All of the predictions were posted, and students were eager to find out if their predictions and tweets were accurate. Triads of students were formed, and each group was responsible for reading their book together and reporting out which of the class predictions were accurate and which were not. Several advanced students were given the option to go to a PBS website (http://www.pbs.org/wgbh/aia/part4/4p2944.html). Their charge was the same as that of the students reading the children's books—confirm or refute the class predictions. They also viewed the National Geographic site on the Underground Railroad (http://www.nationalgeographic.com/railroad/) and prepared to lead the class through the interactive site.

After the report outs were finished, each group constructed their own definition of the Underground Railroad and formulated three questions they wanted to ask the docents during the field trip. One final activity helped the students put the ordeal of escaping to Canada in perspective. The students went out to the track oval and walked a mile, and each student kept track of how long it took him or her. Then they figured out how many miles they could walk in ten hours. Back in the classroom they each picked a slip of paper out of a box. On the paper was the name of a town in a former slave state. Their job was to research the distance between that town and the Canadian border and then figure out how many 10-hour-days of walking it would take them to reach freedom.

Visuals, physical activity, text, background information, and collaborative work prepare the students for a purposeful fieldtrip. These experiences designed to build prior knowledge are also setting the stage for a larger U.S. history unit on the buildup to the American Civil War. These students live where there is no oral history tradition of slavery or the plantation system. Building their prior knowledge will help them think deeply about the events and attitudes of our country's past history that still impact our current society.

Science: The second semester of this middle school science class focuses on earth science—geology, climatology, and oceanography. Mr. Andrews knows that to march through the textbook one chapter after another will not only bore his students, but also will provide only a glancing understanding of the major concepts. What to do? Naturally, the first step is to check the standards. The standard relating to the earth reads, "Students will gain knowledge about the earth and the processes that change it."

The key words, "processes that change it (earth)" spawned an idea. Why not create expert groups in the class that focused on one particular aspect of the earth science curriculum—volcanoes, glaciers, weather, etc. All of the groups could work under the umbrella of an essential or guiding question related to the standard, while at the same time, Mr. Andrews would be differentiating by interest and cognitive strengths.

An open-ended, intriguing overarching question would allow gifted students to dig deeper and use more sophisticated sources. He knew he had to craft an excellent question, but he decided to start with "Over time the earth has changed. What can we predict will happen in the near and distant future?" His vision was to work with the students to refine the question and design how the groups would work and how they would demonstrate their new learning by teaching the rest of the class.

But first, Mr. Andrews realized he didn't have a clue what his students already knew, plus he suspected that most did not have enough general knowledge of earth science to make good decisions about what they would like to become an expert in. His next step was to check out his public library for children's books on the subject to start building prior knowledge.

Mr. Andrews staggered out of his local library with a stack of informational children's books related to earth science—*Devastated by a Volcano; Leveled by an Earthquake; The Top and the Bottom of the World; Icebergs, Ice Caps, and Glaciers;* and *Escaping the Giant Wave* were some of the titles. Delighted with the books he had found that would really help his special education and ELL students with vocabulary and visualization, he began planning his approach as he lugged the books home on the subway.

He came up with two ideas for these books, but he needed to enlist his teammates' help. The simplest idea was to just ask his teammates to keep a stack of the books in their classrooms and encourage students to read them when they finished an assignment ahead of everyone or had a few minutes in homeroom. His second idea was to request that they to do a Read Aloud at the end of each of their classes for a week using one of the books he had gathered. He planned to lobby hard for the Read Alouds because all students would hear a variety of books read aloud which will give them more background knowledge. Mr. Andrews decided to pose it as a pilot program for ways the team could support each other's curriculum goals. He will suggest that if it builds prior knowledge for his earth science work, perhaps they could do it again with children's books related to one of his teammate's units. He will further make his case by reminding everyone that they often lament about the end of class being ragged and that this type of activity will help all of them finish class on a positive note.

He found one other book that he was going to save for the opening of the unit—*Hottest, Coldest, Highest, Deepest* by Steve Jenkins. This colorfully illustrated book succinctly describes some of the most extreme places on earth. Jenkins also includes information about related places in the United States and around the world. For example, the highest waterfall is Angel Falls in Venezuela. On the page is an impressionist representation of the falls, plus a map, and a chart comparing the height of Angel Falls to Niagara Falls and the Empire State building. The combination of text and exquisite illustrations will appeal to his students who love words as well as those who need images to help them create mental maps of ideas and concepts.

His opening lesson will consist of reading aloud the Jenkins' book and stopping after each section to have students locate where each geographic feature is on a map at Animaps (http://www.animaps.com/#!home). Because his students don't have a lot of background information about geography, he is going to step outside of his comfort zone and utilize this free website so that his students can explore digital learning aids and become familiar with the location of countries mentioned in the Jenkins book. He knows the interactive nature of the site will intrigue and engage his students because they live in the digital world outside of school.

Figure 5.2 Animap

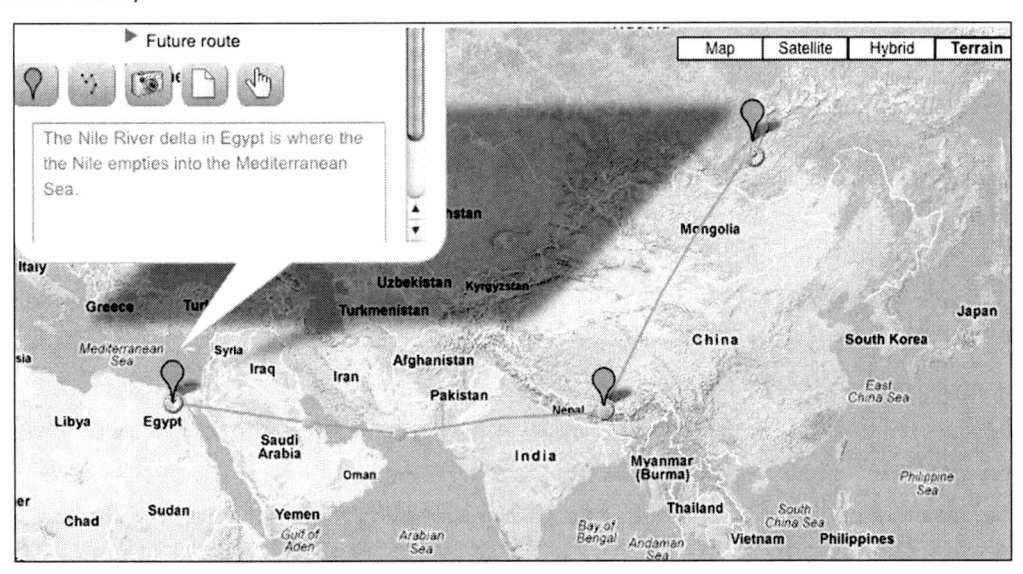

This lesson component of building students' prior knowledge will probably take about a class period because he knows the first time they try out Animaps there will be a learning curve. He will take them to the computer lab where partners will create their own Animaps by adding annotations describing the places mentioned in *Hottest, Coldest, Highest, Deepest* on their digital maps. Next they will use the features of the site that allows users to plan a route from site to site and to animate this route. Sets of partners will share their maps with each other. Mr. Andrews knows this activity could take on a life of its own because the students will want to try out all of the site's possibilities. He will promise time for them to come back and explore this site some more.

The next day he will work with the students to generate a list of earth science inquiry topics suggested by this book and the others they have been exposed to in the team classrooms. Bringing all of the books back into the classroom allows the students to refresh their memories as they pass the books around and peruse them. After a few minutes he will have the students brainstorm topics related to the books. He expects they will amass a long list including glaciers, wild weather, and earthquakes.

Next he will need to take them one more step – to generate inquiry questions based on these topics. He knows he will need to model this process using ideas from the various children's books. He thinks he will hold up *The Story of Snow* and *Snowflake Bentley* and wonder out loud about snowflakes and how and why they are formed. Then, he will take these wonderings and turn them into an inquiry question (see appendix) that he can research. He will think out loud about possibilities and finally suggest, "Why are some winters snowier than others?"

Next he will have small groups of students look at the list of topics the class generated and experiment with writing inquiry questions. It will be hard work for the students, but Mr. A is sure they will persevere with his coaching. He hopes they will come up with questions like *Why are there different types of volcanoes? Why do tornadoes seem to occur only in certain areas of the world? Why are there so many kinds of rocks?* These inquiry questions will become the focus for the expert groups that work together to answer the questions and present their finding to the class. Then to tie everything together, the class will synthesize the information from the different research by responding to the initial essential question, "Over time the earth has changed. What can we predict will happen in the near and distant future?" He needs to spend a bit more time planning that part of the unit because synthesizing is a difficult thing for young adolescents to do. In the meantime, with the help of his teammates and a variety of excellent children's books, Mr. Andrews feels ready to tackle this building prior knowledge activity and his unit.

Benefits

Children's authors and illustrators are expert at taking complex ideas and making them understandable to younger students with concise wording and inviting images. For older students these books with beautifully crafted text and colorful pictures provide the "big picture" or basic information about a topic that is easy to understand. Children's books are not intimidating to less able students and can help them develop vocabulary and background information. The imagery in these books will certainly appeal to the students who find visual supports helpful. Conversations about these books will appeal to many students including those who like to think out loud about ideas. In the past 20 years the children's books industry has grown exponentially and a great variety of texts on a myriad of subjects are now available to the middle level educator who wants to utilize their combination of text and images to help students understand key concepts.

6

Podcasts

Description

This information-disseminating tool of the digital age comes in different formats—audio, audio plus images, and audio plus video. The last two types are often referred to as enhanced podcasts. They are a tremendous asset to educators because up-to-date information on myriad topics is just a couple keystrokes away. Even better is that the only equipment necessary to use them in class is a computer, perhaps an LCD projector (see Appendix) if using enhanced podcasts, and a $20 set of speakers from Radio Shack or Best Buy (if your school does not have any speakers of its own). A podcast is especially helpful in capturing students' interest in topics they know nothing about or fail to see the importance of studying. Created by professionals in the field who exhibit loads of enthusiasm for their topic, good podcasts often connect their subject to what is going on in the world. The other option is for the teacher to create her own podcast.

Students can download podcasts to their home computers as well as their school ones and access the information multiple times. Allowing for the checking of information multiple times in private is a marvelous attribute of the podcast. Often, young adolescents resist asking for information to be repeated in class if they didn't understand it the first time. Access to podcasts solves this problem. Also, a teacher can have students listening to different podcasts at the same time and then share the information with the class. This approach differentiates for both interest and readiness.

To get full impact from the podcast, use it in conjunction with an extended KWL or some other activity that structures how students interact with the podcast. The activity should help students identify the important points of the podcast and provide time for students to discuss the ideas and formulate questions. The other caveat is that deciding to use a podcast on the spur of the moment is risky: anyone can make and post a podcast to the Web, so you must check the source (see Appendix)! Picture doing an astronomy unit and thinking it would be interesting for the students to listen to amateur astronomers talk about the fun of watching the night skies. You listen to the first five minutes of a podcast during your planning period, and it sounds great—you know your students will be intrigued! In class all is going well until minute eight of the podcast when the speaker starts to ramble on about the little green men who came to visit. Whoops! Well, perhaps a teachable moment, but the parent phone calls won't be any fun to deal with. Secondly, sometimes the content is designed for post-Ph.D students and thus, much too complex for middle school students. As with all lesson strategies, you need to estimate how long your young adolescents can remain sitting and focused on the podcast's content; if it's an hour-long podcast, plan on breaking it into parts.

Purpose

- Begin to create mental map with images
- Build interest and elicit student questions
- Begin to build vocabulary
- Introduce background knowledge

How It Differentiates

- Appeals to the digital learner
- Provides an introduction to new vocabulary and is especially helpful for students who lack a general background knowledge
- Supplies visual learners with images to connect to ideas, events, locations, and vocabulary (enhanced podcasts).
- Offers different levels of complexity in the way material is presented
- Allows multiple experiences of the same information so students can listen/view as many times as needed without being embarrassed

Procedure for Teacher

1. Explore podcasts on your own! Look for topics that interest you outside of school. For example, fly fishing has several sites with podcasts. Making something your own through personal interest builds confidence in using a tool. Here are some ways to find podcasts.

    - iTunes, a free download no matter what computer you are using
    - Google "topic + podcast"
    - Podcast.com for education: http://education.podcast.com/
    - Podfeed.net: http://www.podfeed.net/

2. Learn how to download the files. Usually it is a matter of clicking where it says "Click here to download." They are called MP3 files and can be downloaded to computers, smart phones, iPods, and iPads.

3. Once you are comfortable with this tool, start looking for podcasts related to your subject area. Check out iTunes U on iTunes.

4. Introduce your students to podcasts by having them listen to something of high interest. For example, iTunes has NFL podcasts. Not everyone will be familiar with podcasts. Ensure all students are proficient with this tool before using it for instructional purposes. This activity could be done in advisory or homeroom. Get your teammates to help—then they will be able to use podcasts in their classes too!

5. Locate podcasts on your topic or create your own (see Appendix).

    - Garage Band on Macs
    - Audacity for PCs at http://audacity.sourceforge.net/

6. Download them to your computer.

7. Make sure you have a sound system to ensure everyone can hear the podcast. External speakers for a computer can cost as low as $20.

8. Design your instructional plan for using the podcast. Some things to think about:

    - Will all students listen to same podcast or will multiple podcasts be used?
    - What is the hoped for outcome? What information will students need to get from this podcast?
    - How will students record information from the podcast?
    - How will this part of the lesson be processed, and how will you know whether or not students understood what they heard?

9. How this activity might be designed:
    - The class is going to be studying the 1930s. Students will read *Roll of Thunder, Hear My Cry* as well as other texts about that era. Born in 2000, these students can't image life without TV, microwaves, online shopping, credit cards, and video games.
    - Everyone will listen to the National Public Radio podcast "Survivors of the Great Depression Tell Their Story". (http://www.npr.org/templates/story/story.php?storyId=97468008) With external speakers attached to a computer with Internet access, the entire class easily can hear the podcast.
    - The hoped-for outcome is that students will begin to build a mental picture of life during the Great Depression—how it affected families and individuals.
        - Students will discuss the title—why the word "survivor"? That's a strong word. Using a Think-Pair-Share strategy (see Appendix) would work well to involve everyone in the discussion.
        - Students will take notes on a graphic organizer.

Figure 6.1 *Great Depression (GD) Graphic Organizer*

Great Depression (GD) Graphic Organizer					
Person	How GD affected family	How GD affected the individual	Long-term effects on the person	Questions?
1.				
2.				
3.				
4.				

- Stopping after each story will allow students time to jot down some notes and any questions that pop into mind.
- At the end students will compare notes, make some generalizations about the 1930s, and then generate some questions based on those generalizations.

Content Examples

History: The eighth grade is just finishing its study of the founding of the colonies in North America and is transitioning to study the events leading up to the American Revolution. The two social studies teachers have decided to add a twist to the traditional curriculum. The overall plan for the year is to look at major events from the different perspectives of the people involved so that the students begin to develop a sense of the forces that drove decisions in the past and still impact the present.

They find online a series of podcasts entitled *Great Moments in History*. One of the podcasts, "The Road to Revolution", showcases four highly vocal individuals sounding off on events just prior to the American Revolution. One is an activist (Sons of Liberty) and others include a rich Tory merchant, a British official, and a revolutionary leader. They discuss a variety of issues in individual segments:

- Funding for the French and Indian War
- The Battles of Lexington and Concord
- Defending the frontier
- Taxation without representation
- The Boston Massacre

In each of their classes, the teachers briefly introduce the characters from the podcast. They ask students to sign up to be on one of the character's "staff". They explain the role of staffers as information gatherers, policy developers, and advisors. Each student knows which staff they are serving on, and they sit together as they listen to the podcast. Each staff selects a "Chief of Staff" who will be the spokesperson for the group.

The teacher stops the podcast after each segment and asks the students to individually summarize the points made by "their guy" and then pair up to share ideas. Next, each staff meets to identify two of the most important ideas that might become "talking points" for their character at a later date. Each Chief of Staff presents the ideas, and the teacher records them on a big chart or class wiki. The process continues through all of the segments and an advance organizer is developed in the form of a chart shown in Figure 6.2 summarizing the major points of the podcast. It can be viewed as a big chart or on the class wiki.

Figure 6.2 Example of advance organizer.

Summary of Major Points in Podcast "The Road to Revolution"				
Issue	Point of View of Sons of Liberty	Point of View of Tory Merchant	Point of View of British	Point of View of Revolutionary Political Leaders
French & Indian War				
Lexington & Concord				
Defending the Frontier				
Taxation Without Representation				
Boston Massacre				

The information on this giant advance organizer will help students stay focused on the big ideas as they read other sources to find out more details. This scaffolding will be especially helpful to students who struggle with reading and identifying what's important and what's not.

The students will stay in character throughout the unit and become experts on their particular perspective of the American Revolution. Naturally, at the end of the unit, the class will synthesize the information and develop a common understanding of the themes and driving forces of the Revolution.

The highly verbal students who love to argue are engaged in this activity because most of them ended up as Chiefs of Staff and are given an opportunity to use their debating skills. By using a Think-Pair-Share model for students to reflect upon the information they have just heard, the teachers give the internal processor quiet think time and the external or social processors an opportunity to think out loud about the important ideas. Furthermore, by breaking the podcast down into small chunks, students who have difficulty sorting through large amounts of information can focus on just one idea at a time. Visually posting the summarization of the big ideas provides scaffolding and a road map of ideas that will wind through the entire unit: taxation, decision makers, representation, grievances, etc.

Science: Genetics is a fascinating subject that engages many eighth graders. However, Mrs. Morgan always has a few that complain that the topic is *so borrrrring*. This year she is looking for a hook that will grab everyone's attention. Cloning is a hot topic in the news, and one that most people don't really understand. She decides human cloning will be her hook. A close look at cloning will take students into the subject of genetics, and using that entry point, she will design lessons to address the appropriate standards.

She has four students in her class who love science of any kind. They do experiments at home and are reading all sorts of science-related materials on their own. She suspects that they are already knowledgeable about genetics, so she gives them the final assessment for the upcoming unit during a study hall. As she expected, they already could demonstrate mastery of most of the standards for the genetics unit, so she decides to compact the curriculum and create a challenge for them: research and debate for the class the benefits of cloning. This debate will provide background information for the rest of the class and, hopefully, raise some issues they will want to learn more specific and accurate information about. Thus, she is differentiating for interest and intellectual capacity. She asks them to come see her during homeroom to talk about the project. She outlines what she is thinking and the four students enthusiastically sign on. They talk a bit more about how they might frame the debate motion and decide to keep it simple: Human cloning should be banned forever. The four students choose sides and plan their research.

During class while the rest of the students are finishing up the current unit, these four will be searching for information on cloning. Because they have already finished the requirements for this current unit, their homework will also focus on this debate. Mrs. Morgan suggests they look for podcasts on cloning as a first step. She mentions that they might check out the Naked Scientists Podcasts entitled "Cloning, Chimeras, and Stem" (http://www.thenakedscientists.com/HTML/podcasts/show/2007.10.28/). She explains to them that this group of British scientists writes and publishes these podcasts for the general population. She reminds them to double-check who is presenting the information so they know it is reliable. The four students are pretty savvy searchers and start by searching *cloning + podcasts + middle school*.

During their time in class, they locate four promising podcasts and assign themselves homework—each of the four will listen to one of them. The next day they compare notes during their work session in science class. One reports that his podcast was so technical that he couldn't understand any of it. That particular podcast is crossed off the list of possible resources. They go through the other three and find that two have possibilities for being usable resources for them. Together they listen to one of the podcasts, stopping and restarting as necessary. They come up with some facts and loads of questions for further research. Mrs. Morgan checks in with them on their progress, and they finalize their plans for the next day. Mrs. Morgan loves having a bank of computers in her room because she can have small groups working on different materials while she works directly with others. She can supervise and coach the small groups more easily than if she had to send them to the library. She does yearn, however, for the day when each of her students has a digital device.

The four students continue to work all week on their research and their arguments are starting to take shape. They use the information from the podcasts as well as other types of resources. The day of the great debate arrives. Mrs. Morgan begins by asking the class to do a quick write about what they think of human cloning. Students share some of their ideas. Then she plays a SchoolTube video of the movie trailer for *Clone 16*, the story of an adolescent who inadvertently learns to clone himself. He is able to slough off all of his unpleasant tasks onto his clones until he creates Clone 16, who has homicidal tendencies. At the end of the clip, she asks them what the underlying assumption in the movie is about cloning. There is a lot of silly chatter, but eventually one student says, "Human clones emerge fully developed, not as infants." The class agrees that's probably not the case. At this point, she asks the students to generate a list of the perceived benefits and drawbacks of human cloning, which is another activity that gets students thinking about the topic of the upcoming unit.

Finally it's time for the debate that is a much-simplified version of the National Debate Tournament format. Each side presents a 3-minute opening statement. Then, they each have 2 minutes to respond to the opposing side. The rest of the class follows the arguments closely using a graphic organizer to note the arguments for each side and to help them make a decision about which group was more persuasive. Mrs. Morgan has the debate videotaped because she plans to turn it into a podcast so that her students add to the information available to others on the Web. At the end, the class votes for the argument that resonated most with them. Because this is a highly charged subject with ethical and religious overtones, Mrs. Morgan is careful not to suggest one argument is the correct one. She wants her students to be thinking critically about this bioethical issue, one of many they will face in their lifetimes.

The next day when the class comes in, they review the information they heard previously and begin to list questions for which they need answers to really understand the issue of cloning. As the questions emerge, it becomes clear to Mrs. Morgan that almost every aspect of her genetics unit falls under the umbrella of the students' questions. She will work in the important unit information not particularly related to students' questions at appropriate times.

In this scenario several students built prior knowledge for their classmates through debate. They used podcasts that provide current and often late-breaking scientific information. These intellectually talented students who were ready to move ahead were able to so without reviewing material they had already mastered. The podcasts gave the teacher flexibility because she did not have to be the provider of the information. She could play the role of coach and clarifier when necessary. The other students received an interesting and thought-provoking introduction to this next unit. Questions generated by the debate will engage the class as they delve into the intricacies of genetics. The four debaters who now understand the basics of the cloning debate will be able to study more diverse topics within the genetics framework, perhaps using additional podcasts. Committed to customizing learning to each student, she will work with these four to identify which standards each of them would like to work on.

Music: The students in the sixth grade general music class have been learning to compose electronic music in the computer lab. Mr. Perez wants the students to demonstrate through performance what they have learned. He is going to have the students make podcasts of their original compositions and/or an explanation of some aspect of composing/performing that will be posted on the school's website. First, however, he wants them to think about the criteria for an effective and enjoyable music podcast. Fortunately, he has inexpensive headsets from the Dollar Store for each computer, so he can have students listening to different examples of music podcasts without bothering their neighbors.

He asks the students to listen to three specific podcasts on the *Kids Music Planet Podcast* and *Kids Talk Radio Podcasts* websites. If the school server doesn't go down, they can access the podcasts online and through iTunes. Because the school server is notoriously unreliable, especially when he is depending on it, he has a back-up plan. He has downloaded the three podcasts and can play them through his sound system if need be. However, part of his objective is to help his students become familiar with iTunes and to use it efficiently. He's collaborating with the teachers in other subject areas on this goal because many of them also use iTunes U for curriculum materials. They are working together to provide students practice with this digital tool in multiple contexts.

The students' task is to listen to the three podcasts and rank them 1-2-3 in quality. They also need to have two to three reasons for their rankings using specific evidence from the actual podcasts. When the students are finished, he has them share their findings and reasons. With this information they set criteria for an exemplary podcast:

- The topic is made clear to the audience.
- The introduction hooks the audience.
- Explanations are specific.
- Explanations include music examples.
- Correct vocabulary is used.
- Voice-overs are easy to understand and well-rehearsed.
- Sound quality of the music is crisp .
- Everything flows smoothly—no gaps of dead air.

The students have constructed their guidelines that might eventually form the beginning of a rubric. They have a prior understanding of what will be needed to be successful in this assignment as well as a couple of exemplars to refer to when necessary. This information is especially helpful to students who have no previous experience with performance or public speaking. These students will also profit by listening to their more experienced classmates discuss the pros and cons of specific attributes of public performances. The experienced students are given an opportunity to clarify their thinking on the subject. By listening to examples of music podcasts, students experience the process rather than just reading about it. Certainly students who learn best through experiential learning will benefit from this activity.

Benefits

Podcasts afford students access to the most current information and opinions on every topic studied. They can provide common foundational information that new learning can be built on. Or, different podcasts on the same topic varying in point of view or complexity can be used to meet specific learning needs or interests of the students. The storytelling format of many podcasts introduces vocabulary in context, brings historical figures to life, and provides real world examples of ideas and skills to be studied. These podcasts that can be listened to multiple times help make rich curriculum resources available to students who have lacked assess to them in the past because of reading, language or vision issues. Transcripts are usually available for the hearing impaired. Furthermore, the enhanced podcasts provide images and text which help the visual learner begin to build or expand their mental maps of a topic. Podcasts bring the world to the classroom and help make learning relevant.

Skits and Other Kinesthetic Activities

Description

Total physical response (see Appendix), a method language teachers use to help students learn a second language, involves the entire body in the lesson. The same idea applies to skits and other kinesthetic activities used as methods of accessing and building prior knowledge. A kinesthetic approach certainly addresses the learning needs of the group of students who have trouble concentrating when they have to sit still for extended periods of time. Depending upon whose research one reads, kinesthetic learners make up from 15-30 percent of our students.

Performing skits; building models; creating pictures, shapes and booklets; and simple movement are examples of kinesthetic activities. When such an activity starts a unit, it can be referenced to help students retrieve and connect ideas as the unit progresses. "Let's look at the models we built when I challenged you to create 4-, 5-, 6-, and 7-sided figures. Let's match them to pictures in the text and begin to learn their geometric names." or "Pull out your foldable books (see Appendix) on types of sentences. Use it to double-check whether or not your essay meets the criteria for sentence variety."

Kinesthetic activities also bring a change of pace and novelty to the classroom. Because novelty positively stimulates their brains, young adolescents remember ideas associated with the experience. Furthermore, kinesthetic activities engage students who possess dramatic, artistic, or athletic flair. Such opportunities allow them to be the stars when often they are overshadowed in class by their peers with linguistic or logical-mathematical tendencies. If, indeed, 15–30 percent of our students enjoy learning through physical movement, shouldn't our classroom activities reflect a similar percentage?

Purpose

- Build interest and elicit student questions
- Make an emotional connection with the subject to be studied
- Create concrete images associated with a concept
- Build schema or mental maps of the concept

How It Differentiates

- Allows students who are oral processors to think out loud
- Provides visual and verbal explanations for the concrete thinker
- Appeals to students who enjoy learning through physical movement and artistic representation
- Offers all students an opportunity to use their creativity
- Removes the pressure of reading and writing from students who have learning differences
- Gives ELL students an opportunity to practice their English vocabulary in a non-graded situation

Procedure

1. Think about your upcoming unit or lesson and identify a major concept or a particular aspect that might be difficult for students to master. Some examples include:
    - Literacy themes in short stories, novels, and poetry
    - Adaptation in a biology unit
    - Exponents and exponential growth
    - The five themes of geography—movement of ideas
    - Emotional intelligence

2. Design a short kinesthetic activity that demonstrates that concept in some way.
    - Relate an idea or concept to the typical teenager's life. Suppose an upcoming literature assignment has the themes of power struggles in relationships, envy among siblings, and loyalty in friendship. Small groups might create skits about teenage life as they relate to those themes. Students will have no

problem acting out confrontations between parent and child, sibling rivalry, or problems involving friends. After each skit is presented, the audience tries to figure out what the theme was. The teacher then shares that these three themes will be evident in the upcoming class novel, and that they will be looking for evidence of what the author's message is concerning those themes.

- Create a physical task that represents the concept or idea. For example, to teach adaptation in biology, a teacher might set up a series of physical tasks—move an object from point A to point B, build a tower, recreate an image through verbal instructions, etc. Then, she would have students partner up and handicap each of the students in the pair in the same way. Some pairs would not be able to use their hands, others could not talk, and a third group would be blindfolded. The partners then would attempt to complete task 1. Those unable to complete the task would be eliminated. Then, those remaining would try Task 2, and so on. At the end, the class would talk about why some sets of partners were successful at certain tasks and others were not. When appropriate, the teacher would introduce the concept of adapting to new situations. "Sarah and Tisha couldn't use their hands to move the box, but did you notice they adapted by using their noses instead?"

- Involve students in a real life demonstration of a concept. Students start the study of representative government by attending a local school board or selectmen meeting or watch one on local access cable TV. Armed with a graphic organizer to help them take notes on procedures, topics, and outcomes, the students would see firsthand representative government in action. They would have concrete examples to relate to the descriptions in their text.

- Incorporate manipulatives that students can use to create, build, or represent a concept or idea: pipe cleaners, poker chips, blocks, paper and markers, etc. For example:

  — Create foldables (graphic organizers that can be manipulated— http://www.dinah.com/) with students to help them see relationships, use as checklists, or to take notes in during the unit.

  — Use pipe cleaners for students to explore which geometric shapes can support the most weight or to construct physical models of shapes for which they will be calculating perimeter, area, and volume.

3. Implement the activity.

4. Process the activity with the students with questions such as
    - What did you notice?
    - Where else in everyday life would you see…?
    - What might be important to remember?

Content Examples

Language Arts: Mr. Wong's language arts class is going to read *The Adventures of Tom Sawyer*. In the past, students have gotten bogged down in the dialect and have had difficulty relating to the characters, who lived in a time and place that modern-day students don't recognize. Keeping them engaged in the novel had been problematic. However, this year, Mr. Wong is going to help students build a prior understanding of several of the novel's themes in a 21st century context. His plan is to give his students a broader appreciation for the story of Tom and his friends by focusing on universal themes of friendship, young adolescent development, a group's unspoken rules, and relationships.

Always struggling with how much time to spend on the accessing/developing prior knowledge components of his lessons, he tends to just jump into an engaging activity. However, past practice has shown him that taking the time to do this stage of a unit well pays off in the end because students are primed with the necessary information for internalizing the new learning.

He begins class by reading aloud Chapter 1, and the class meets Tom, Jim, Aunt Sally, Sid, and a stranger who, of course, turns out to be Huck Finn. There's a great scene in which Tom and the stranger are both full of swagger and try to one-up each other. Aiming to make the scene relevant to current times, Mr. Wong asks for several volunteers to reenact the situation using 21st century language (obviously, he cautions about appropriate language). Ultimately, four boys volunteer and go out into the hall to prepare. With the rest of the class, he does a think-pair-share in which partners think about similar situations they have seen in popular media—movies, TV, shows, music videos. The partners then share their concrete examples with the class. The volunteers then perform their skit which focuses on a football team with a new kid, who was the star quarterback of a neighboring school. He and the veteran quarterback square off to prove who the better player is. After a generous round of applause, the class processes this part of the activity with probing questions:

- What emotions do you think each player is feeling?
- What did they say or do in the skit that makes you think that?
- What are some possible outcomes of the encounter?
- What might be a similar situation in a non-athletic setting? How might the people involved react? What might be the same? What might be different? Why?

Mr. Wong rereads the section that describes Tom and the stranger's war of words. He asks the same questions that he used with the modern situation:

- What emotions do you think the characters are feeling?
- What words or actions from the story make you think that?
- What are some possible outcomes of the encounter?

After the discussion Mr. Wong directs the students to a chart where he has the characters' names they have met so far: Tom, Aunt Polly, Sid, the stranger, and Jim. Under each name, the class lists what they have learned about each character so far. Mr. Wong is confident now that the students have a handle on the main characters, and he will continue to add to the chart as they go deeper into the story. This chart will help the more fragile readers keep people straight.

The students will be reading independently in the future, and fortunately, the novel is in the public domain. Students can download a free audio version from Librivox (http://librivox.org/). Each student will have access to the text no matter his or her reading ability. Because students will download the audio version of *Tom Sawyer* to their own digital devices (iPod, computer, phone), they can listen any time and as many times as they like. Earbuds in place, they can even listen on the school bus or subway. In the past, poor or slow readers who had trouble with Twain's use of dialect and vocabulary could not participate in classes reading *Tom Sawyer* or other great works of literature. They were often given low vocabulary/high interest books that are rarely rich in character or plot development. Now, these students have equitable access to classes that will build their critical thinking skills and their academic background knowledge because, thanks to audio book sites, memorable texts can be read and heard.

But Mr. Wong is not quite ready to send them off to read independently. He wants to further scaffold by building awareness of some of the big ideas that discussions will focus on in future classes. He divides the class up into groups of three and four. Drawing from Mr. Wong's hat a slip of paper with a skit scenario, each group must perform a skit. Scenarios include:

- Conflict with siblings.
- Consequences of breaking society's rules.
- Supporting a friend while defying the adults in one's life.
- The in-crowd and the out-crowd—how's life different for each group?

Delivered among a lot of hilarity, the skits stimulate engaging discussions as the class talks about the big ideas and how they relate to everyone. Mr. Wong writes the words *universal themes* on the board and shares that the class will be exploring these ideas as they read the novel. He states, however, that his premier goal is for them to enjoy this great story; the analysis will only be a part of their work. He assigns them Chapter 2 and sends them on their way.

By the end of the class, all of the students were involved in talking about the underlying themes of *Tom Sawyer*. The skits grabbed the attention of those who needed to move around and to construct something (a skit) to understand. The skits also helped build mind maps of concepts prior to class discussion. Finally, by exploring some of the themes of the novel in terms of the students' everyday experiences, Mr. Wong built in the relevance necessary for those students who really need to know why it matters to study a topic.

Math: Ms. Gupta was watching a retrospective on Marcel Marceau, the famous mime. "Yes!" she yelped as she leapt to her feet. "That's how I will introduce the concept of symmetry." Here was her plan:

> Goal: Students will be able to automatically visualize three different types of symmetry: reflection, rotational, and translational.
>
> Strategy: Use total physical response (like World Languages uses) to create strong visual memories for each type of symmetry.
>
> Phenomena before vocabulary: During this building prior knowledge stage, symmetry vocabulary would not be addressed; that would come after students had experienced the concept.
>
> Formative Assessment: Provide application experience as follow-up to the class activity.

Procedures:

1. After showing a YouTube (see Appendix) video of a mime, she took them outside to the soft, clean grass.

2. All students participated in miming different situations: brushing their teeth, climbing a rope, eating an ice cream cone on a hot day.

3. After everyone was loosened up a bit, she asked for a volunteer to come up and strike a pose of his/her choice that could be held for 5 minutes.

4. Then, another volunteer stood in front of the first student and mirrored the pose. As the two volunteers posed in front of the class, she asked the class to brainstorm words that described the image of the two mimes. Of course, some said, "silly," but others mentioned "image", "reflect", and "copy". Ms. Gupta quickly made a stick figure drawing of the students and charted all of the words to use late.

5. Then, she asked the second student to hold the pose while moving around next to the first, so that both students would be facing the same direction. Next, she asked for three more volunteers to come up, join the line, and hold the same pose. Once again, she asked the students not miming to brainstorm words describing the scene. "Repeats," "multiples," and "pattern" emerged as some of the descriptors. Once again, Ms. Gupta recorded the words under a stick figure drawing for later use.

Skits and other Kinesthetic Activities 93

6. She thanked the volunteers for participating in that part of the activity and asked for a different volunteer who wouldn't mind stretching out on the nice, clean, soft grass. Up popped Tommy, who immediately fell face down on the grass. Ms. Gupta asked him to turn over and mime that he was holding off a large flat stone that might crush him. She then asked others to join Tommy on the ground and get in the same pose as if they were spokes of a wheel. One last time, she sketched a stick figure image and asked students to brainstorm descriptive words for this tableau and then duly recorded them.

7. The class went inside, and Mrs. Gupta gave them their homework. Pointing to the charts, she instructed students to look for five examples of similar scenes in the world around them. They could either sketch them or use their phone or digital cameras to capture the images. They needed to note on piece of paper or a note app on their phones where each image was shot and whether it was a part of something bigger.

8. During the next lesson, Ms. Gupta would introduce the correct vocabulary for each form of symmetry. Using the students' own words from the charts, the class would be able to list the characteristics of each form and then share real-life examples from their homework assignment. The total body response aspect of the prior knowledge activity would engage the boys and girls who like to move as they learn. Students lacking strong spatial skills also would be helped by these life-size models. Symmetry is a visual concept, and the multiple visual representations would help all students internalize the concepts as they move through this particular unit.

Science: In a professional development workshop, Mr. Holmes had learned a new strategy, ABC/CBV or *activity* before *concept, concept* before *vocabulary*, which fit in with his philosophy of inquiry learning. His classes were in the middle of unit on cells, and he was about to teach the new concept of permeability. In the past, students had had difficulty pronouncing the word, let alone truly understanding the concept. Their misconception was to picture the cell wall or membrane as something solid such as a brick wall. Plus, there always seemed to be a question about permeability on the state science exam, and too many students got it wrong. This year Mr. Holmes was determined that they would get it right.

Suspecting that several students might already understand the concept of permeability, he decided to do a very quick pre-assessment using a Ticket Out the Door. During the last four minutes of class he handed students an index card and asked them to write down or draw everything they knew about permeability as it applied to cells. He explained that this wasn't a test and that he just needed to know who already knew something about this topic. As he suspected, two or three students in each of his classes understood the concept. They had either sketched a picture of the process or written a pretty good definition on the card that compared favorably to the expected answers on the state test.

Thinking about the ABC/CBV model led Mr. Holmes to think about activities that would help the rest of the students understand the concept of permeability. He wanted students to see that some materials let liquids pass more freely than others. Rounding up empty gallon jars from the cafeteria and large, heavy-duty elastic bands from the office, he got help from the Consumer-Family Life teacher in listing several kinds of fabric to purchase for his permeability activity. He also was mulling over some possibilities for those students who already understood the concept of permeability; he would develop an appropriate instructional plan for them.

When the students arrived the next day, their worktables were already set up with equipment. Those who had been able to explain permeability were directed to the bank of classroom computers that had been turned into a learning station. The directions at this station had the students go to the Cells Alive (http://www.cellsalive.com) and Biology4Kids websites (http://www.biology4kids.com/files/cell_main.html). Their activity for the next two days would have them digging deeper into the specifics of permeability. They needed to design an Xtranormal (http://www.xtranormal.com/) animated presentation for the rest of the class on what they learned. He was very confident they would master Xtranormal on their own. His students were always showing him new tools and apps they were "playing" with outside of school. He plans to monitor them during class and use email to check in on their understanding of the websites on cells. He will also set up a Skype conference with each group after school to check on their progress. He knew he could just get them together during study hall or home room, but they loved using Skype. Mr. Holmes thought back to the days before he had easy access to computers and how difficult it was to provide meaningful work for advanced students. He probably would have given them a choice of topics related to cells but not covered in the middle school curriculum and had them do a mini-research project. They could have worked in the room or the library, and he would have checked in with them during homeroom or study hall.

The rest of the students found large gallon jars with different types of fabric stretched across the tops and secured with an elastic band on their worktables. Each jar was labeled with the type of fabric that covered it. Next to the jars were beakers with different liquids in them; the beakers were also labeled. Directed to treat this activity like a regular science lab, students were to predict what would happen when they poured the liquid into the jar through the fabric. Because the conditions at the work stations were different, each group would visit all of the tables. While students observed and carefully recorded what happened, Mr. Holmes would coach and ask probing questions as he circulated among the tables and the computer learning station.

The work groups shared their data, and Mr. Holmes worked with them to summarize their findings. Obviously, one of the things students noticed was that although all the jar coverings were made of fabric, some allowed liquid to pass through more easily than others. Also, if the liquid had anything in it besides water, there was residue left on most of the fabrics. The class ranked the fabrics according to the ease that water penetrated them and ran into the jar.

Mr. Homes knew that making comparisons is an effective way to internalize a concept. His aim was to help the students understand that some walls or barriers, though seemingly solid or designed to keep material out, often allow some substances through (permeability). He showed the class a picture of the only cribstone bridge in the world and asked them how it was like some of the fabrics covering the jars (see Figure 7.1). Some of the similarities students noticed included that there was a pattern, it could support other objects, and it was made by people.

Figure 7.1 Cribstone Bridge Harpswell, Maine, 2011

Suddenly the lights went on and students began to see other similarities:
- It's a barrier in the water, but it also lets water go through it.
- It keeps objects in the water from going through like boats and whales just like the fabrics kept the sand and other materials in the water out of the jar.
- Some things, like small fish, can get through. The open weave fabric on the jars let small stuff through also.

"Well done!" remarked Mr. Holmes. "We will apply what we saw today to the structure of the cell tomorrow." Although this seemingly simple lesson had taken a class period, he was sure that it was worth the time because the students had experienced and thought about the basic characteristics of permeability, even though they hadn't been introduced to the technical vocabulary word. He also had all of the charts with the students' observations and summary statements. By taking time to build a mental map for his students of the conditions in barriers that allow some substances to pass through them, he was confident that the lesson on the permeability of a cell membrane would be easily understood by all of his students. They would then be receptive to their classmates' presentation on some of the more technical details of permeability. These small groups of advanced students in each class remained engaged and not bored as they developed a short, animated movie to share what they had learned. Furthermore, Mr. Holmes now had three Xtranormal experts in each class for when the entire group used that tool in the next unit.

Benefits

Middle grades students spend a lot of time sitting in their chairs. A kinesthetic activity immediately changes the pace and routine of the class and grabs the attention of the students. They talk, they move, they create and begin to generate an enthusiasm for a topic. The process builds concrete experiences and background information that can be referred to throughout the unit. *Remember when we created a wave of dominoes crashing onto the table? How was that action like this wave action we are looking at now?* Making connections assists students to internalize new information and will be especially helpful for ELL students and others lacking a broad academic vocabulary. Students with dramatic or artistic or musical interests often discover a way to exhibit their talents during a kinesthetic activity and become engaged in the ideas of the unit. Skits and other kinesthetic activities bring variety and interest to a lesson as they help students access background information that will aid in their learning.

Slideshows and Videos

Description

Powerful images "… create visual frameworks. When students are able to build onto these visual frameworks, either by connecting the material to previously known concepts, or by building new ideas on top of them, learning takes place. That's the power of slideshows or videos" (Elliot, 14). Because today's students have grown up in a world rich with images combined with music and text, it makes sense to use the energy produced by such experiences to hook students as they begin a new unit. Use what MTV and YouTube already know—multimedia encounters keep people's attention. In addition, the images combine with other experiences in and out of school to build students' schema or mental models of what they need to learn. New information must connect to something already known if the retention of knowledge is the desired outcome.

Visuals help make abstract ideas more concrete for our early adolescents who have not yet transitioned completely to formal cognitive operations. They also level the background knowledge playing field for those who lack opportunities to travel and explore the world through varied experiences beyond the brick and mortar of their neighborhoods. Images also inspire curiosity. Imagine seeing a picture of a pyramid or a spiral galaxy or the highly poisonous funnel-web spider of Australia for the first time! Questions just seem to tumble forth—How did they build that? Why did they build it? Why doesn't the galaxy fly apart?

Finally, images tie the past to the present for students. What can we learn from the rise of unions in the 1800s and 1900s to help us understand labor issues today? What are the similarities between the impact of the Industrial Revolution on society and the impact of the Information Revolution today? What do the fashion trends through the years tell us about the changing roles of women and children in society?

Purpose

- Build interest in a topic and elicit student questions
- Help students begin to create a mental map of the ideas that interconnect within a concept
- Begin building vocabulary
- Introduce background knowledge

How It Differentiates

- Appeals to students who learn well through images and music
- Introduces vocabulary and concrete images to students with language issues, ELL students, or to those with limited background knowledge
- Engages students who relate to new learning through the digital world
- Pulls in students who respond to an emotional reason for learning
- Interests students who are easily bored in school

Procedure

1. Search the web for suitable material related to the concept on which you will focus; suggested sites are in the chart shown on the next page. If you can't find what you want, it's relatively easy these days to make your own slide shows with images, text, and music on the web with Animoto (http://animoto.com/) or SlideShare (http://www.slideshare.net/). Images provide a powerful entry point to new learning, and the digital world opens possibilities for the teacher unimaginable ten years ago. Even if you are a neophyte, you can use images in your classroom to inspire, illuminate, and illustrate important ideas and concepts. The following chart includes helpful slide show tools, images, and video resources.

Searching for Media	
Type of Media	**Place to Search**
Free Slide Show Tools	Animoto: http://animoto.com/ Slide Share: http://www.slideshare.net/ iPhoto (Macs)
Images	Flickr's Creative Commons section: http://www.flickr.com/search/?q=Creative+Commons&f=hp Pic4Learning: http://pics.tech4learning.com/ Wikimedia Commons: http://commons.wikimedia.org/wiki/Main_Page
Video	YouTube: http://www.youtube.com/ TeacherTube: http://www.teachertube.com/ Wikimedia Commons: http://commons.wikimedia.org/wiki/Main_Page Movie trailers at iTunes: http://trailers.apple.com/trailers/ Film Clips for Character Education (cost involved): http://www.filmclipsonline.com/ If your school blocks video sites, convert them using http://www.zamzar.com/ at home to a format you can use on a school computer (.mov)

2. Don't let the blocked sites at school slow you down! Learn to use Zamzar (http://www.zamzar.com/) on your home computer to convert Internet video to a format you can use at school (.mov). There are only four simple steps to take, and you can download a video at home and put it on a thumb drive to show at school.

3. Create a lesson plan that asks students to identify ideas, words, questions, people, events, etc. that the images bring to mind. Record student responses on charts or a wiki to reference during the unit. There are lots of ways to organize such lessons; here are some things to consider:

- How will the images you choose help students engage with and understand the upcoming lesson better? How will they build or access prior knowledge?
    - Make connections between the unknown and the known: Will seeing pictures of the Coliseum or other ancient arenas allow students to make connections with modern sports venues such as Gillette Stadium, Lambeau Field, or Candlestick Park and thus help them better understand the magnitude of the ancient world's architecture?
    - Provoke strong emotions: Images of the devastation left by the 2011 Japanese tsunami, the leveled forests following the eruption of Mount St. Helens, or the inundation of New Orleans after hurricane Katrina certainly will cause most students to be awestruck by the power of the forces of nature and lead to many wonderings about the release of that power.
    - Create a mental image to connect with a new vocabulary word: Many students have never seen a larva, geodesic dome, or hexagon. They don't know where Boston is in relationship to Chicago or understand what "abundance" or "currency" mean. Showing them pictures will build the foundation for increased understanding.
    - Empower students to take action by showing them examples of other young adolescents who have impacted their world: Google "teen philanthropists" or "teen entrepreneurs" to find a variety of sites showing how teens have successfully taken the initiative in working toward solving a social problem.

        Middle grades students do relate to the pain of others and want to find ways to help. Often, a chance to come to the aid of others will lead students into a deeper understanding of issues with societal impact. For example, helping to raise money for a food pantry might include speaking with the pantry directors about the depth and causes of hunger in their community that could lead to a class discussion about the role of government in solving social problems.

- How will you and the students process the images and make the connections to the upcoming lessons?
    - Small group discussions
    - Journaling with words and images through notebooks, blogs, tweets, or wikis

- Interviews with family members or friends who are familiar with the topic
• How will you capture the students' thoughts, questions, and new insights?
    - Chart paper
    - Class wiki
    - Google docs or other collaborative online writing tool
• When and how will you return to the students' thoughts and questions during the unit?
    - Use them as a base of inquiry projects.
    - Post charts in the room or maintain class wikis with student notes and questions, returning to them regularly to add information.
    - Assign students as guardians of each question with the responsibility to record the information the class uncovers and report out at the end of the lesson or unit.

Content Examples

Math: Mrs. Cavanaugh was determined that her students were not going to ask her this year, "Why do we have to study math? We never will use it outside of this class!" She decided to access and further build their prior knowledge about math in the real world right at the beginning of the year. She found a series of videos on YouTube called *The Born Numeracy* (http://www.youtube.com/watch?v=olwE5mZJ-Fk) that are obviously a takeoff on Matt Damon's *Bourne* movies. These 3-minute videos take a fast-paced run through a cityscape challenging the viewer to find as many examples of mathematics in the real world as possible.

Mrs. Cavanaugh first had students brainstorm a list of topics they had studied in math over the years. "Fractions! Percentages! Geometry!" echoed throughout the room. She recorded all of the terms on the board and then stepped back. "OK—we're going to watch a video. Your job is to jot down as many specific examples of math in the real world that you see in the video. Let's limber up those digits—wiggle your fingers and shake out your hands! Are you ready? Here we go!"

She played the video, and the students watched for a moment before they remembered to start looking for math in the world. Fingers flew as they scribbled notes. Too soon it was over, and the students asked her to play the video again. She agreed.

Afterward, she asked the students to share what they had seen. Recording their answers under the topics they had brainstormed earlier, she had to add additional topics including symmetry, patterns, and measurements as they went along. Some of the responses included:

- Geometric shapes like rectangles in buildings and bridges
- Prices—in decimals
- Percentages of fats and sugars on food labels
- Identical shapes repeated in a pattern

When they finished, they had over fifty responses sorted into nine categories. Starring the topics they would be studying this year, Mrs. Cavanaugh promised they would make real world connections to all the topics. As an optional homework challenge, students could make videos with their phones or digital cameras similar to the one they had just seen. She suggested they pick one of the starred categories like fractions or geometry and film examples of them in their homes and neighborhoods and at sporting events and other activities. Because she was beginning to plan for her students to create digital books full of mathematical problems from their world to solve, she also asked them to start keeping track of anything mathematical they saw that they didn't understand.

Knowing that many of her students were digitally savvy, she thoroughly engaged them in activities connected to the Internet. She also recognized that she was helping to review math vocabulary for students who struggled with math or had expressive language issues.

Science: Studying volcanoes was always interesting to his students, but Mr. Miller knew that many of them had never seen a hill higher than Hoosier Hill, ten miles south of the school. He found that using a slide show before the students starting reading their textbooks helped them begin to build a mental map that helped them understand the terms and concepts related to volcanoes.

Searching the Web, he found a variety of images related to volcanoes—charts explaining the different types, maps of the Ring of Fire, and actual photos of volcanoes around the world. After downloading the images, being careful to also record the attribution information so he could model ethical searching, he put them in a slide show format and set them to Johnny Cash's "Ring of Fire" (see Appendix).

Dividing his students into three groups, he gave these directions.

- Group One: watch the video and jot down vocabulary words that might be important. Some of the slides included specific volcano-related words such as shield volcano and magma, and students could copy them.
- Group Two: record any questions that come to mind.
- Group Three: write down what you notice. The class had been working on developing their skills of observation, especially during labs. Mr. M. thought that asking students to record what they noticed would give him feedback on how well their skills in this area were progressing—an informal formative assessment. He played the slide show once and gave the students in each group time to share information and talk about it. Then he showed it again and asked them to add to their initial notes.

After the second showing, each group met again, finalized their notes, and then reported out. Using the words that the vocabulary group gathered, Mr. Miller created a word wall that the class would add to and reference throughout the unit. He knew that his students needed between 15-30 encounters with new vocabulary to internalize it.

He also recorded their questions and their observations to skillfully weave these into future lessons. He planned to leave the charts up so that the less able readers could quickly double-check what important ideas they should concentrate on as they read.

All of the students, not just the well-traveled ones, could connect their reading to the volcano-related images they had seen. They could picture the snow-capped cone of Mount St. Helens and the fiery lava flows from Kilauea. The illustrations of the Ring of Fire had generated questions such as "Why there and not here in Indiana?" In addition, the student-generated questions would focus lessons, a surefire way to engage students in class activities.

Art: The Art Department was preparing for their semester-end show, and this year Ms. Rossi and Mr. Feldman decided to have the students themselves devise the installation. They are going to incorporate the process in a mini-unit on interior design. The art teachers have access to class sets of iPads, which make museums of the world just a finger swipe away for every student. By using the iPads, students would have access to a variety of galleries and have exposure to world-class ideas about mounting an art show.

The teachers created a Portaportal (http://www.portaportal.com/) site (see Appendix) that had direct links to a variety of virtual tours of many of the worlds' outstanding museums. In class students had the choice to work in pairs or by themselves exploring the different sites. They were asked to visit at 3 different sites using a separate note taking guide for each one.

Figure 8.1 A Portaportal Site of Virtual Museum Tours

▽ **Museum Tour**
- Smithsonian
- The Louvre
- Museo Galileo--Florence
- Hermitage
- The Tate
- Metropolitan Museum of Art
- National Gallery--London
- Museo Reina Sofia--Madrid

After the students finished this activity, in larger groups they shared their notes and identified some big ideas that they might use in the student exhibition. They also formulated several questions about exhibits that they wanted to research further.

Virtual exploration of the different museums helped even the playing field of general knowledge about museums and art gallery exhibits. Through virtual tours, students who had not yet had the opportunity to travel and visit museums were able to see several famous exhibit halls up close and personal. Furthermore, students whose learning is enhanced by visual components and those who like to talk about what they are learning were especially engaged in this activity.

Figure 8.2 The note taking guides were in an easy-to-use chart format.

Gallery Exploration	
Name of the Gallery:	**Location of the Gallery:**
Things to Look For:	**Notes:**
Description of the Installation • Type of art displayed • Setting • How art is displayed—pedestals, on the wall, suspended from ceiling, etc.	
Ways information about exhibit is displayed	
Interesting ways space is used	
Colors that are effective in displaying the exhibits	
Strategies for lighting the displays	
Other observations about making art visually pleasing	

Benefits

Videos, slide shows, and virtual tours allow students and teachers to push through their classroom walls and visit places that are awe-inspiring and beyond their experiences. A student from the deep South who has never experienced a blizzard is going to have difficulty relating to Jack London's "To Build a Fire" in which it gets so cold one's spittle freezes in the air before it hits the ground. Show them a video of dogsled teams slogging through a blizzard during the Iditarod races in Alaska, and they begin to understand the impact of the setting of this great short story. Disturbing images of the Dust Bowl or concentration and relocation camps help students understand the ravages of the Great Depression and the results of war on civilian populations. Images generate interest and questions, both which are apt to lead to higher level of student engagement. Beyond providing background knowledge and motivation, these activities also provide students with a preliminary understanding of key vocabulary and perspectives on the big ideas they will be studying. Everyone can participate in an activity rich in images and audio—poor readers, good readers, deep thinkers, visual learners, hearing or visually impaired learners, ELL students, and those with short attention spans—because the ideas do not hide in written text that is often indecipherable to some and because images and sound often illicit a strong emotional response.

9

Student-Generated Webs

Description:

Webs, also called concept maps and mind maps, show how pieces of information are related to one another. In this chapter we will simply use the word web to denote this type of graphic organizer. Below is the beginning of a web about the state of Maine that a student has constructed. Maine, the foundational topic, is in the center and is surrounded by several subtopics: industry, geology, history, and vacationland. Supporting details are connected to the subtopics. Although there are many gaps, the web does indicate what this student already knows.

Figure 9.1 Example of Webs, Concept or Mind Maps

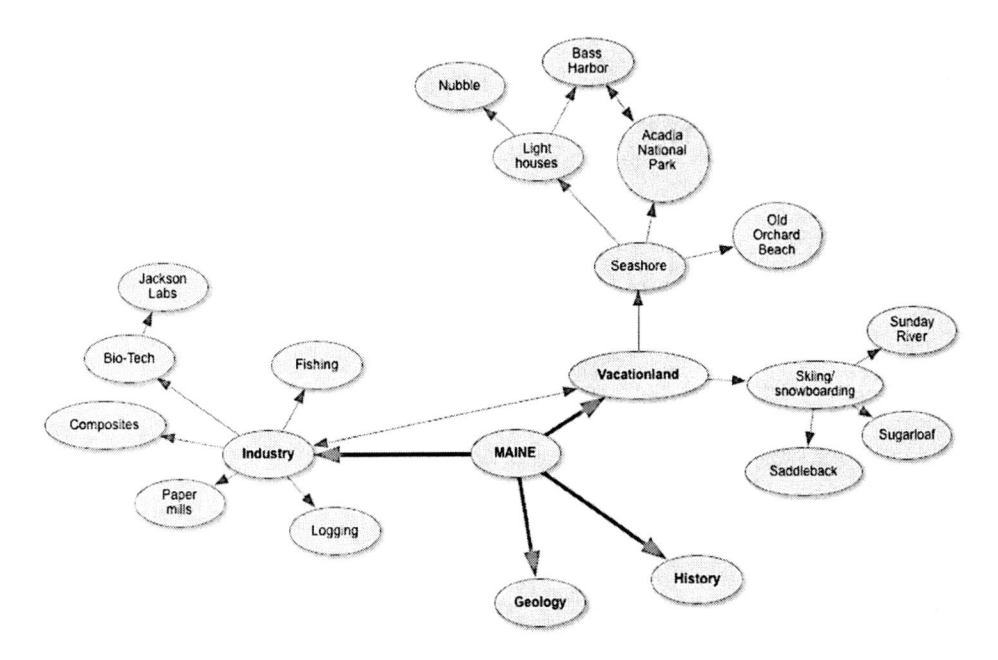

The benefits of making webs is that students can show relationships and hierarchies by using arrows and lines, colors, and different sizes of text and text features. For example, in the Maine web, Vacationland is shown as a subtopic because it is such a major part of life in Maine. However, the web maker also recognizes that activities such as skiing and visiting the ocean attract visitors, which creates another industry. So a double-headed arrow is used to show that relationship. Webbing allows for non-linear thinking similar to the way many people use the Internet—jumping from an article to other sites via links. The digital natives who are our students often respond to webbing's flexibility and visual representation. Because of these attributes, webbing is an effective tool for digitally-literate students to access and display prior knowledge. Also webbing engages students who have difficulty expressing themselves using the written word. Using words and perhaps images and arrows rather than sentences and paragraphs allows them to more easily demonstrate what they already know.

Using webs has another advantage! How often have teachers and parents heard the response "Nothing" when a young adolescent is asked what they learned? If the same webbing activity is used at the end of the unit, students can compare their individual webs and see concrete evidence of learning. In the Maine web there was no prior knowledge demonstrated about the history of Maine. At the end of the unit on Maine studies the history section would look something like Figure 9.2 on the next page. Pre and post-unit webs provide evidence of learning for students, family, and teachers.

When using webs as a way to access and build prior knowledge, the teacher can have the students work independently or in small groups. That decision depends on the teacher's purpose and future instructional plan. Student webs can also be combined into a class web and used to

- Keep track of the learning.
- Generate questions that might drive a portion of the work.
- Make connections with what has already been studied.

Using the Maine example, it would be instructive to compare portions of it to a similar web about U.S. history in the same time period. Students could

- Compare and contrast trends in Maine history with what was happening elsewhere.
- Make generalizations using the two webs.
- Practice synthesizing information from different sources.

Figure 9.2 Example of Post-unit Webs

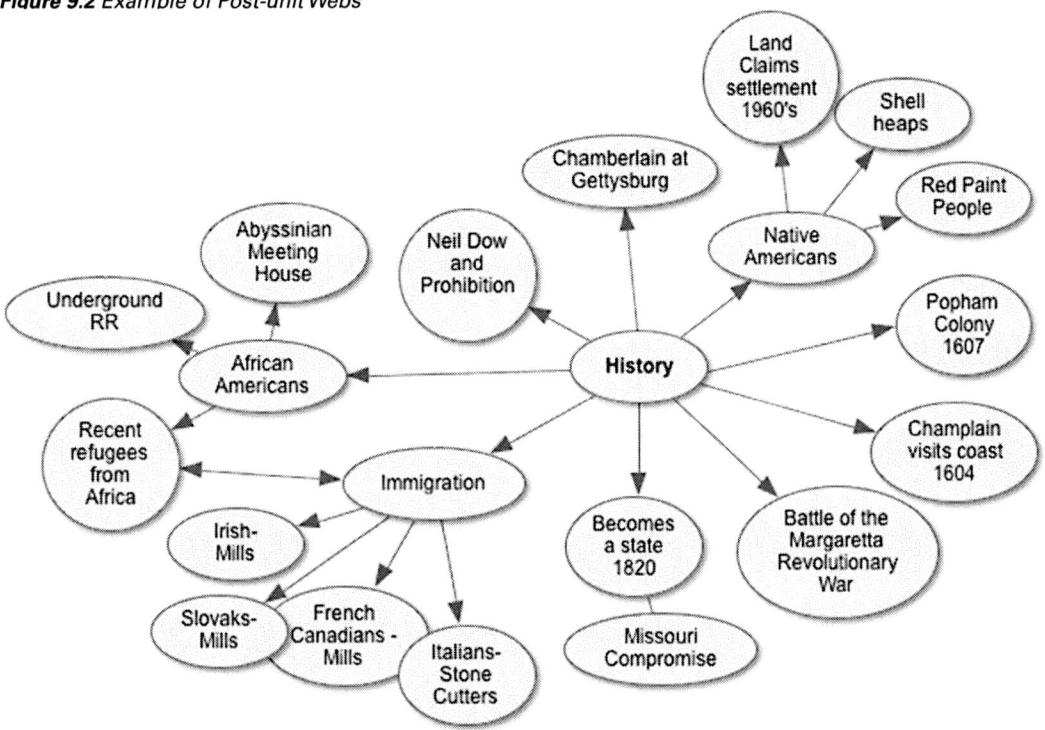

One last thought. Some people absolutely hate webbing just like some students find traditional outlining as counterproductive to the way they process information. Take time to talk with your students about various ways to take notes and organize information. Explain that you want them to try a variety of approaches, so they will learn which method works best for them. If you see students getting frustrated with webbing (lots of start-overs, scratch-outs, and scribbles), take time to have a one-on-one chat to see if you can help them figure out what is keeping them from completing the assignment. Have one or two alternative suggestions for completing the assignment. Examples are using a simple jot list or writing ideas on separate index cards and arranging them afterward in a logical manner. Keeping a digital camera handy in the classroom allows you to take a picture of index card arrangements, thus providing a record of the student's work.

Purpose

- Ascertain the level of student prior knowledge
- Build interest and elicit student questions
- Begin to build understanding of the relationships and hierarchies within a given concept or topic
- Provide evidence of learning at the end of the unit

How It Differentiates

- Allows students with writing difficulties to express what they know graphically
- Appeals to tech-savvy students when digital tools are used
- Provides teachers an opportunity to gather information about what students already know and misperceptions they may have.
- Introduces students with gaps in background knowledge to vocabulary and relationships among ideas when the webs are shared

Procedure

1. Before asking students to web what they already know about a topic, share a model with them so they can picture what you expect them to do. It's always wise *not* to assume they already know how to construct one. Providing a skeleton web with the major subtopics listed will give students a little forward momentum. Listing the subtopics ensures that students address the information critical to understanding the unit. There are a variety of ways to create the webs:

    - Paper and marker
    - Free online webbing tool like Bubbl.us (https://bubbl.us/) and ReadWriteThink Webbing Tool at (http://www.readwritethink.org/classroom-resources/student-interactives/readwritethink-webbing-tool-30038.html).
    - Commercial digital webbing tools such as Inspiration at http://www.inspiration.com/ or OmniGraffle at http://www.omnigroup.com/products/omnigraffle/.

2. Collect and review webs to help fine-tune the unit. Evaluating student webs using a couple of criteria helps you identify what information students just need to review and on which concepts they will need extra instructional time.

- Identify student misconceptions. Are students using words incorrectly or misidentifying items? For example, in a geography unit: does everyone know the difference between countries and continents? In a geology unit: do students believe that dinosaurs and humans walked the earth at the same time?

3. Identify unexpected gaps in crucial background information by first listing for yourself the prior knowledge students need to be successful in this unit. If evidence of those ideas is lacking in the webs, figure out how to provide students with the necessary information.
4. Save webs so students can add to them.
5. Halfway through the unit return them to students and have them add to the web using a different color marker or text.
6. Collect and use individual webs as a formative assessment. Look for corrections and additions on the webs. Have countries previously identified as continents been relabeled correctly? Have students made adjustments to misinformation about geological eras? In addition, identify
    - Areas students still don't understand and that need reteaching.
    - Important information students have failed to web, so it can be revisited and taught in a different way.
    - Ways to use information to group and regroup students in order to address specific learning needs through small group instruction and review.
    - Students who may be ready to move at a faster pace than their peers.
7. At the end of the unit, return webs to the students to have them use a third color to add yet more information to the webs.
8. Ask students to reflect on what the webs show. Questions might be:
    - What are three big ideas you have learned that you did not know at the beginning of the unit?
    - What questions do you still have?
9. Add the webs to students' portfolios as evidence of learning.

Content examples

Spanish: "¡hola!!" Señora Silva greeted her eighth graders on the second day of school. They had studied Spanish in both sixth and seventh grades. Señora Silva was new to the school, and although she had reviewed the curriculum, she did not know to what degree students had mastered it. She was especially interested in their knowledge of verbs. Modeling what she wanted students to do, she created a graphic organizer in a web format. The web conjugated the verb hablar (to speak) in the present tense.

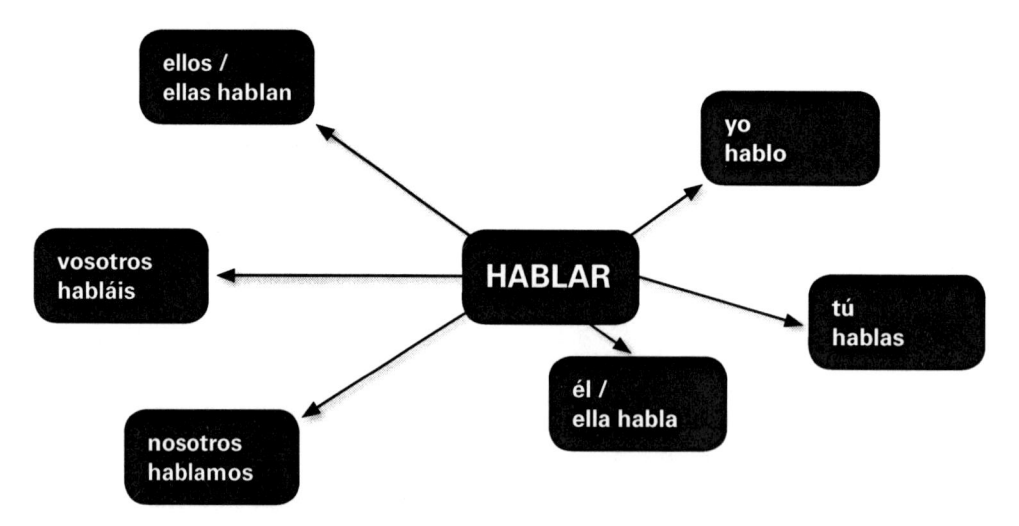

```
            ellos /
            ellas hablan
                                        yo
                                        hablo
    vosotros
    habláis            HABLAR
                                        tú
                                        hablas
            nosotros      él /
            hablamos      ella habla
```

She then distributed 18" x 24" newsprint paper and black markers to the students. They copied her model and then added 3 verbs they remembered. They also conjugated (listed the verb forms for I, you, he, etc.) them as well as they could. Stressing to the students that they needed to work independently, Señora Silva felt confident she was obtaining an accurate picture of her students' knowledge of verbs, and she collected, folded, and stored the charts for later use.

When it was time for mid-quarter progress reports and student-led parent conferences, she returned the charts (hablar and their 3 additional verbs) to the students along with green markers. She asked them to add to their original charts any additional verbs they had mastered and correct any errors they could find. Immediately seeing the progress they had made in learning Spanish verbs, most students noticed their charts had more green than black writing, and they felt a sense of accomplishment. Students added the charts to their Spanish portfolio that they would share with their parents during student-parent conferences. The charts would provide students with evidence of progress to show their parents.

Using this non-threatening strategy to access students' prior knowledge and skill acquisition appealed to the students. Because the emphasis was on looking at personal improvement rather than a comparison to others, students felt empowered. For many shy or less confident students, the ability to show their knowledge in a graphic way rather than just in recitations was a relief. Señora was working on building their confidence as Spanish speakers, but she knew it would be a long process for some. In addition to helping the students, the charts were valuable references for her planning of whole class and small group activities because they provided the data she needed to group and regroup during class.

Advisory: Shasta team teachers were meeting with the other seventh grade team teachers (Rainier, Hood, and Denali) to discuss the focus for the next semester's advisory time. Concerned about bullying, they were reviewing options. Ms. Shirokawa wondered what the students' experiences with bullying might be. "A lot goes on we are not aware of," she said. "And…I'm not sure all students would be real honest while sharing in a public forum like advisory group. What can we do to identify their real concerns about bullying?"

Mr. Marcos, a science teacher who uses concept webbing extensively in his class, suggested that perhaps the students could individually web what they knew about bullying and their concerns. "It would make it easy for everyone to communicate with us, especially those who are shy or find writing difficult or like to express themselves visually. We could look at the webs and identify the things we need to address during advisory and reinforce in our classes."

The group next identified what information they wanted to draw from the students about their perceptions of bullying. They decided to use a two-step process. Step 1 would be an engaging partner activity giving everyone some common language; they would share and discuss results with the entire class. In Step 2 students would work independently.

Step 1: After finding partners and gathering drawing paper and markers:
- Partners web their definition of bullying. Teachers suggest that students consider what bullying looks and sounds like as they construct their web. People's names are not used in the web unless they are characters from books, the media, or the news.

- Pairs share their webs, and the advisory group begins to define bullying in seventh grade language. The teachers expect this definition will change as they work through the advisory program.

Step 2: Working independently, students web responses to the following questions:
- What does cyberbullying look like in our community?
- What are the dangers related to bullying? For the victim? For the bully?
- Where are the hot spots for bullying in our school?
- In what ways have you experienced bullying—personally or as an observer?

All the teachers agreed to encourage students to add related topics that were important to them. As the team suspected, when they looked at the student-completed webs, they were able to identify many topics for the upcoming semester's advisory plan. They also discovered several spaces in the area of the school that needed more adult supervision because many students mentioned them as hot spots for bullying. The student webs were saved for use later in the spring to see whether or not student perceptions and attitudes were changing. Eradicating bullying was going to be a long process; however, the webs provided the teachers with specific information to address the real needs of their students and to make their teaching most effective.

Social Studies: Ms. Beaulieu likes to emphasize the "wisdom of the class" with her students. She enjoys saying, "All of us is smarter than any one of us." Therefore, when she began her unit on the United States Constitution, she decided to have her students create a class web using her Smart Board. The web would be saved to her computer and added to during the unit.

As she reviewed the unit, she designated the big topics to be part of the web.

1. The Compromises
2. Executive Branch
3. Legislative Branch
4. Judicial Branch
5. The Bill of Rights
    - Free speech
    - Freedom of religion
    - The right to bear arms

6. Other amendments
7. Student rights

Her classes were much larger this year, but she didn't want to give up on cooperative groups. She created a separate group of three or four students for each topic and had them web on their computers what they knew about it using Popplet (see Appendix), a free tool on the Internet. They would be responsible copying and pasting their work to the class web. Chatting and encouraging groups as they worked, Ms. Beaulieu helped each group identify what prior knowledge they possessed. Because she knew students heard a variety of interpretations and misinformation on TV about the Constitution, she was very curious to find out what the students believed.

While the class silently read two articles about Supreme Court decisions on requiring students to say the Pledge of Allegiance in school, the groups one at a time added their parts to the class web on the Smart Board, which she saved to her computer.

After a spirited discussion about the articles, she refocused the students on the web they had created on the Smart Board. Of course there were many more gaps than facts, but she assured the class that they would fill them in as they progressed through the unit. Ms. Beaulieu was easily able to identify misconceptions the students held, and she made special note to address those throughout the unit. Having participated in the making of the web, all the students were now able to see where the unit was going and to begin building their constitution-related vocabulary with words like executive, amendment, and legislative. Ms. Beaulieu emailed the web to ELL and special education teachers and promised to send them updates as the class added information. They would be able review and reinforce big ideas and vocabulary with their designated students. She also sent it to the teacher of the gifted and talented who responded immediately with several ideas on how she might be involved in the unit. Ms. Beaulieu also decided to post the initial web on the wiki she had set up for parents and families and explained she would post updates so everyone could track the students' progress in learning to understand the U.S. Constitution. Much to her surprise, several parents with background in the law and government offered to come in and work with students.

As the unit progressed, Ms. Beaulieu would pull the web up on the Smart Board and ask the group responsible for each section to add new information they were learning. At the end of the unit she emailed the file to each of her students, so they would have evidence of their learning and a great study guide for the test.

Benefits

Webs quickly provide a visual map of the ideas and important vocabulary early on in the unit. Learners who like visual supports to help them make sense of new information find webs very useful. Also, below-grade-level readers can use the web developed as a prior knowledge exercise for a reference to help them keep track of the important ideas they need to focus on throughout the unit. Furthermore, all learners benefit from seeing how words and ideas are related to one another; understanding the relationship and hierarchy among words helps students internalize their meanings more fully. Web 2.0 webbing sites add flexibility to the activity since it is easy to rearrange the parts of the web, color code related ideas, and add images to support understanding through images of examples. All of these attributes of digital webbing sites support learning for the majority of the students because they can use the accouterments of the site to personalize their webs. Webbing helps organize ideas and concepts visually. The teacher can see what students understand and what they do not. Students have a foundation of ideas they can elaborate on in written or multi-media presentations.

Word Sorts

Description

This activity focuses on key vocabulary words that students must know to understand unit or lesson concepts. Students either receive a list or stack of words on index cards from the teacher or they brainstorm their own list of words they associate with a specific topic. For example: *Please list all of the words you can think of related to weather.* Depending on the teacher's purpose, the students would do one of two things:

1. Group the words they think go together: rain, sleet snow; tornado, hurricane; climate change, ozone, etc.

2. Sort the words into groups that indicate how well they know the word. *I know it well! I have an idea what this word means!* Or *I don't have a clue what it means!*

Word sorts enable teachers to note for which words they will give whole-class direct instruction and for which words they will give smaller group instruction. This strategy can be done digitally, with pencil and paper, or with manipulatives. Students can work individually or in groups. In groups, students lacking background information or having less developed literacy skills can hear *how* their classmates think about the words. This metacognitive process models for everyone a variety of thinking processes.

Word sorts allow students to access their prior knowledge; see which words are most important for the next unit; and in some cases, have their first encounter with new vocabulary. Often, it's a good idea to pair the written word with an image to help students, especially visual learners, begin to build a deep understanding of new words. Remember, students need to *hear* the word pronounced correctly, see the word written, and when possible, *associate* it with an image. Also, seeing words in a graphic arranged to show the relationships among them is helpful.

Below is a partial list of words related to the study of biomes and two examples of word sorts using these words.

Biome Words

rainforest	temperate	fen
desert	canopy	chaparral
tundra	arid	oasis
grasslands	permafrost	savanna
taiga	boreal forest	tropical

Figure 10.1 Word Sort Example # 1 Determining Depth of Knowledge

Determining Depth of Knowledge			
Directions: Sort the words on your vocabulary list into the following categories			
I don't have a clue what this word means!	I think I've heard of this word, but don't ask me to define it.	I'm pretty sure I know what this word means.	I know this word so well I could teach it to others!

Figure 10.2 Word Sort Example # 2—Exploring How Words Are Connected

Exploring How Words Are Connected					
Directions: Place the words on your vocabulary list under the biome label to which they are most related					
rainforest	desert	tundra	grasslands	taigra	temperate

Notice that word sorts can also be used to show evidence of learning. Students will see evidence of their academic growth if they do the same word sort at the end of the unit and compared it to the initial one. Save the first word sort—whether it is a piece of paper or a digital photo of a physical sort, so students can compare it to a later one.

Purpose

- Build interest and elicit student questions
- Ascertain level of student prior knowledge
- Build vocabulary
- Create an artifact that shows evidence of student learning

How It Differentiates

- Affords an opportunity to group students by interest or knowledge level. For example, if there are two or three students that know a lot about the topic, they might form one of the groups and receive a slightly different set of words.
- Supplies students with language issues (ELL, small vocabularies, dyslexia) an early introduction to new words they must master. They will see the words written, hear them spoken, and in some cases connect an image to the written word before they come across them in a textbook or website.
- Provides opportunity for students to work independently or in groups.
- Allows the teacher to gather information that will help determine which words/concepts to emphasize in her instruction and whether students have misconceptions about the concepts in the upcoming unit.

Procedure

1. Identify key vocabulary and concept words for the unit. Be discriminating with this list! It's not reasonable to expect students to learn 50 new words over a two-week unit. Use the standards that will be addressed and assessed to help guide the process of choosing. Remember: it takes 15-30 significant encounters with a new word before any of us are able to develop a deep understanding of it. Which words do you want to spend that much time on? For example, when studying geometric shapes, it is more important that students understand "polygons" than that they are able to define "dodecahedron".

2. Create an activity in which students sort words into categories and/or identify which words they know and do not know. Students might work independently, in small groups, or as an entire class. The activities might be paper and pencil or flash card manipulatives or digital. Here are four examples:

- Index card sort #1: give individuals or partners a stack of index cards with a word written on each one. Ask students to sort them into categories. The teacher can easily see if students recognize the relationship among the words and any misconceptions that exist.

- Index cards sort #2: give individuals or partners a stack of blank index cards and ask them to brainstorm words they associate with the upcoming unit. Each word goes on a separate card. Then the students sort them into categories. The teacher can identify which words the students recognize as being related and any misconceptions that exist. Students are also demonstrating what they already know about the topic by the words they are able to generate.

- Individual identification of words students know, kind of know, and know for sure #1: provide students with a list of the words they will be responsible to know and a handout similar to the one below. This activity can be digitally adapted by creating charts and spreadsheets. When the teacher collects the words, he can easily see which words are going to be problematic and which ones just need a review.

Figure 10.3 Individual identification of words #1

Totally unfamiliar words	I sort of know these words when I hear or read them.	I know these words well!
perceive *attribute* *impose*	*equate* *ethnic* *prior*	*final* *label* *predict*

- Individual identification of words students know, kind of know, and know for sure #2; create an online survey with questions like the one in Figure 10.4. You will receive the results in a chart that graphs the answers in a way that tell you in a glance the degree to which the words are familiar to students.

Figure 10.4 Individual identification of words #2

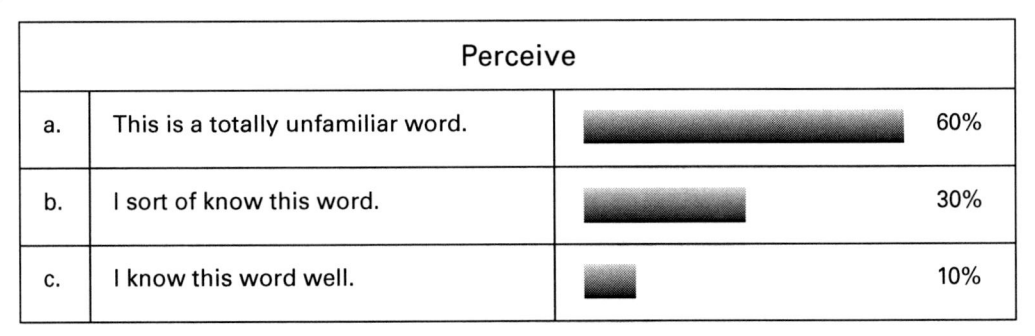

	Perceive		
a.	This is a totally unfamiliar word.	▓▓▓▓▓▓▓▓▓▓	60%
b.	I sort of know this word.	▓▓▓▓▓	30%
c.	I know this word well.	▓	10%

Use the same activity at the end of the unit to chart student progress. Students will be able to see which words they have moved into the "I know these words well" column or how much more easily they categorized key words and identified the relationships that connect the words.

Content Examples

Language Arts: Ms. Rideout begins the year with a word sort strategy she adapted from Janet Allen's *Words, Words, Words* to find out what suffixes and prefixes students know. It's an initial formative assessment to help her plan her vocabulary lessons for the year.

She gives students a worksheet with the year's suffixes and prefixes such as the one shown in Figure 10.5. After she reads aloud the suffixes and prefixes, the students individually fill in the worksheet. She wants the students to see and hear the prefixes before they begin because some students may recognize the prefixes when they hear them; and others, when they see them. They are reminded that no grades are attached to this activity, and the information will help Ms. Rideout plan good lessons. She doesn't want to bore students by reteaching prefixes and suffixes the students already know. She is, however, a savvy teacher and knows that students sometimes over- or under-estimate their knowledge or skill level. She will note any inconsistencies in the student-self-assessments with other evidence she has related to students' language proficiency. Helping students take responsibility for their own learning is an important goal of Ms. Rideout's, and she knows they have to practice using and reflecting on self-assessments in order to develop that particular characteristic of being a good student.

Figure 10.5 Prefix activity

Below is a list prefixes. I expect you know some, have heard of some others, and have not heard of many of them. Please sort them into the appropriate column.			
Ante, anti, com, contra, dia, dis, extra, hemi, hyper, hypo, inter, intra, non, post, pre, pro, re, semi, sub, trans, un, under			
Don't have a clue what this means!	I've heard of it, but wouldn't want to define it.	I know this prefix so well I can teach others what it means.	Definitions of prefixes I know are in this column.

Ms. Rideout has created a collated chart to help identify with which prefixes students are unfamiliar, which they need to review, and which they may have mastered. She will make a similar chart for the required suffixes. Needless to say, she will double-check whether or not students truly can apply their knowledge of prefixes and suffixes they say they know during the short vocabulary practices with which she normally starts class.

Figure 10.6 Collated prefix activity results

Prefix	Not a Clue	Heard of It	Know It	Instructional Notes to Self
ante	✓✓✓✓✓✓✓✓✓✓✓✓✓✓✓	✓✓✓✓	✓✓	Teach
anti	✓✓	✓✓✓✓✓✓✓✓✓✓✓	✓✓✓✓✓✓✓✓✓✓	Review
com	✓✓✓✓✓✓✓✓✓✓✓✓	✓✓✓✓✓✓		Teach
contra	✓✓✓✓✓✓✓✓✓✓✓✓✓	✓✓✓✓✓✓✓	✓✓	Teach
dia	✓✓✓	✓✓✓✓✓✓✓✓✓✓	✓✓✓✓✓✓✓✓✓✓✓	Review—did math teacher teach it?

She will repeat this process several times during the year to check students' progress in mastering the required prefixes and suffixes. Believing it is important for students to see progress, she shares her chart with her students using a transparency of the chart and an overhead projector. Because there are no names attached, no one feels uncomfortable with everyone seeing the data. This year she thought she might set class goals with the students for shifting checks to the right in the columns. During the fall semester she will have students redo the sort, and then she will compile the new results. It will remain anonymous because the subsequent charts she shares will just have the data displayed. She sets goal 1: *the I don't have a clue* column will be empty of checks by January 1. Of course, she will double-check the self-reporting with a formative assessment. She is curious to see how students will react to this goal setting. If it works well with the class as a whole, she will think about adding individual goal setting during the spring semester.

Ms. Rideout has also written these prefixes on the word wall that the class will continually review. With the word sort activity and the word wall, she is helping her students with poor vocabulary knowledge build their sight and spoken word banks. Because of these activities, they will become more cognizant of word structure as they read. Helping students achieve at higher levels is linked directly to their breadth of vocabulary knowledge.

Science: Ms. Morrison's class is beginning their unit on the systems of the human body. There is a lot of vocabulary associated with this unit, as there is with all of the topics in the seventh grade science curriculum. She wants a general assessment of the class's prior knowledge, so she is going to use a word sort activity in which students generate the words.

1. First, she explains that they will be using a think-share process. After a short time of thinking independently, they will share their ideas in a small group.

2. Next, Ms. Morrison asks each student to make a list of the words they associate with the structure of the human body. Setting a time limit of two minutes, she asks students to aim for at least 10 words.

3. Then she puts students into groups of three and gives each group a stack of blank index cards. Because she wants students with less background knowledge exposed to new words very early in the process, she makes sure the groups are heterogeneous. She instructs each group to share their individual lists and write a separate index card for each word that appears on someone's list. She likes the think-share procedure because it gives the students who need more time to process tasks or ideas some quiet moments to think. She also recognizes that some of her students thrive on the social aspect of learning, so the sharing time fits their learning needs.

4. Once the stacks of index cards are completed, she models what she wants the class to do next. She asks one group to give her the top five cards on their stack.

lungs	bones	stomach	stomach	brain

5. She explains that the next step in the activity is to group words in ways that they seem to go together. "For example", she says, "bones and backbone seem to me to be connected so I am going to put them together like this."

bones	backbone

"Lungs, stomach, and brain—well they are all inside of the body, but I bet there are better groupings. Does anyone have a word they think goes with brain?" Several hands go up waving index cards. "Nerves" and "Thinking" are on the cards. Ms. Morrison takes the cards and puts them in a column with the brain card. She then asks the groups to categorize their cards in a similar manner. The students put their heads together and busily arrange and rearrange cards.

6. Ms. Morrison calls time and hands each group several blank index cards. She asks them to come up with labels for each of their word groups.

7. When everyone is finished, Ms. Morrison takes digital pictures of the groups and their index card groupings as a record of the groups' work. As she walks around, she makes notes on what students seem to know, any misconceptions, and the obvious gaps in knowledge.

8. She shares this information with her students. "It looks like this group has a pretty good understanding of the skeletal and circulatory systems, so we will just have to do a quick review on them. The respiratory system and the digestive system—all of the groups have some major gaps, so we will spend time studying those in depth. And I noticed that no groups had anything about the reproductive system (giggles from the class), so we will also include a close look at it as well as the nervous system. I think you will find the endocrine system interesting because it includes all of the hormones raging through your bodies causing you to grow out of your clothes quickly and the other big changes of adolescence."

The students leave class with the beginnings of mental maps related to the systems of the human body. Students have also had concrete practice in categorizing, a critical thinking skill that they will be using later in the year. Ms. Morrison plans to give her students multiple practices in this skill before it is a required task. Finally, as the students explore this complex unit, the new information they encounter will connect to their fourth grade prior knowledge that Ms. Morrison has helped them access.

Interdisciplinary Curriculum—Physical Education and Health: The Allied Arts teachers want to create a yearlong curriculum for the seventh graders focusing on healthy living. One of their early lessons will be a word sort to begin building word recognition. After brainstorming a list of 40 words that students would encounter through the year, the teachers wrote each one on a piece of construction paper and laminated them so they could be reused many times.

When the Health and Physical Education classes met together in the gym, the teachers handed each student one of the words. Then they flashed a graphic of a football field up on the screen.

Figure 10.7 Example of Football Field Graphic

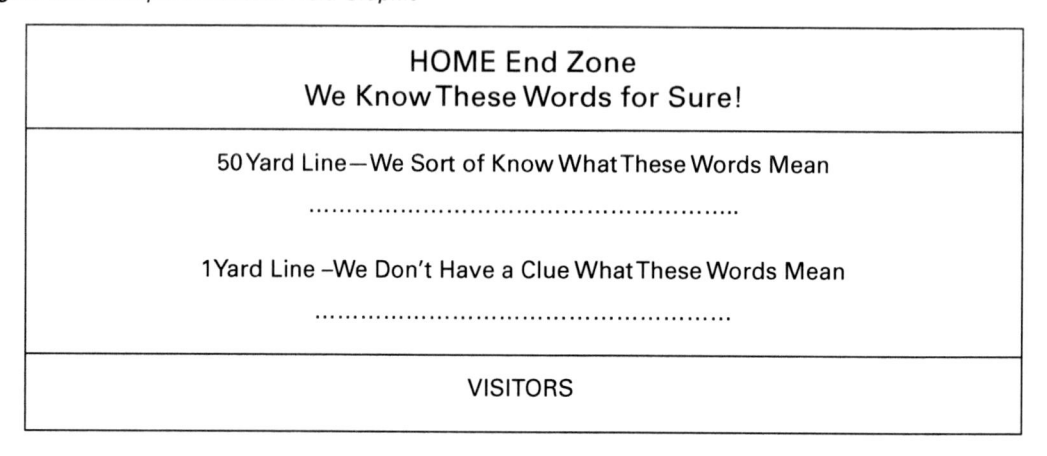

HOME End Zone We Know These Words for Sure!
50 Yard Line — We Sort of Know What These Words Mean ....
1 Yard Line — We Don't Have a Clue What These Words Mean ....
VISITORS

The teachers explained that students would place their words on the 1-yard line, the 50-yard line, or in the HOME end zone depending on their understanding of the word. The 1-yard line meant "I don't know the word at all", 50-yard line meant "I have a vague understanding", and the HOME end zone indicated "I can use the word correctly in conversation and writing". Because the teachers wanted to inject movement into the process, students would jog during the activity. The teachers emphasized that it wasn't a race, but that students just needed to keep moving.

The students were paired up and given a couple of minutes to discuss what they thought their two words meant. Each student then decided where he would place his word: 1- yard line, 50-yard line, or the HOME end zone! Then everyone jogged out to the football field. Fortunately there was no wind that day, so the word sheets wouldn't fly off!

Standing in the visitors' end zone, jogging in place, students were reminded of the rules. With a loud tweet from the physical education teacher's whistle, the students took off to place their words on the appropriate yard lines. When a student reached her goal, she put down the word and continued to jog in place while her partner jogged on to his line. Students jogged in place until all of the words were positioned.

With another toot of the whistle, everyone jogged up to the HOME end zone and gathered around the words located there. Students with words in the end zone then explained what their words meant. The teachers were making notes on the accuracy of the explanations. They were prepared to gently step in if any inaccurate information was shared by saying the definition wasn't quite spot on. Then, they would take time to clarify the meaning through student participation. Finally, they would ask the original student to restate the corrected version and let him keep the card. A special note was made of the word so the teachers could revisit it again and reinforce the correct meaning.

Next, the students were challenged to jog back down the field and look at the words on the 50- and 1-yard lines and pick up any words they could move to the end zone. "Toot" and they were off. The class dashed down the field and pulled up at the 50-yard line. They milled around looking at the words, some stooping to pick up a card with a word they knew. Another toot and they raced down to the 1-yard line. Once again, the students looked over the cards. If an individual knew a word, she picked it up. Two minutes later, the physical education teacher called everyone into the end zone. Once everyone was in the end zone, each student with a new word explained it to the group.

By the time the class was over, the students had gotten some physical activity, compared answers with a peer, and been introduced to words they would need to master over the year. The teachers left better understanding what their students already knew. They also could easily identify those who were reluctant to exercise and would need more encouragement and fitness counseling as well as those who had a preponderance of background knowledge and those who did not. This information would help them form cooperative groups and competitive teams.

Benefits

Vocabulary is key to internalizing new concepts and ideas but parroting back definitions does not guarantee an understanding of words. Students need to comprehend multiple meanings and connotations of words and recognize how words are related. For example, representative government is a big concept vocabulary term, and there are many words that help make up that concept—elections, representation, 1-person/1-vote, campaigns, legislature, recall, impeachment, etc. Students need to be familiar with all of these words and know how they are related to understand "representative government". Since it takes most of us 15-30 encounters with a new word to truly internalize it, using a word sort as a way to build and assess background knowledge is an excellent start to the process of mastering critical vocabulary. Not only are students introduced to words, but they also begin to build their mental map of how the words relate and support one another. Because this activity can be done with manipulatives, pencil and paper, or digitally, it can be adapted to the learning preferences of the class. Also, any unit has vocabulary ranging from fairly simple to very sophisticated, and therefore, a teacher can provide individual students with just the right mix of difficulty to push their thinking but not totally frustrate them. Finally, students lacking in experiences that build general academic background knowledge enter school with a large gap in written and oral vocabulary. This gap greatly influences their chance for academic success; therefore, it is imperative that vocabulary study be integrated throughout a unit. As Ludwig Wittgenstein said: "The limits of my language are the limits of my world."

Appendix

Animaps: (http://www.animaps.com/#!home) is a free online site that allows you to annotate maps in interesting ways. Symbols, pop-up text and images, and changeable lines and shapes are all available for customizing your map. The final result is a video that can be sent to others. The home page has examples and a tutorial. This site is very easy to learn how to use, and students will be able to adapt it for most subjects.

Attribution—Checking Internet Sources: Teaching students to check the reliability of their Internet resources is a critical step in the research process. Understanding everything in an URL is important: what do .ac or .net really mean? what do symbols like the tilde (~) indicate? how can you find out who owns a website? November Learning's Information Literacy Resources page (http://novemberlearning.com/resources/information-literacy-resources/) has excellent resources for helping teachers plan lessons to build students' sophistication in searching.

Children's Books: Your local librarian/media specialists and pre-school and primary teacher colleagues can recommend children's books; they know the books and have them available to borrow. Resources are also readily available on the Web and in print. Here are several:

Print
1. *Beyond Words: Picture Books for Older Readers and Writers.* S. Benedict and L. Carlisle, editors (1992) Heinemann.
2. *Companion to American Children's Picture Books* by C. Kirk (2005) Greenwood.
3. *A Critical Handbook of Children's Literature* by R. Lukens (2006) Allyn & Bacon.

4. *Inviting Children's Responses to Literature: Guides to 57 Notable Books*
   A. McClure and J. Kristo, editors (1994) National Council of Teachers of English.

5. *Neal-Schuman Guide to Recommended Children's Books and Media for use in Every Elementary Subject* by K. Matthew and J. Lowe (2002) Neal-Schuman.

Internet

1. *Children's Literature:* http://www.childrenslit.com/
2. *Databases of Award-Winning Children's Literature:* http://www.dawcl.com/
3. *Carol Hurst's Children's Literature Site-Curriculum Pages:*
   http://www.carolhurst.com/subjects/curriculum.html
4. *Children's Picture Book Database at Miami University:*
   http://www.lib.muohio.edu/pictbks/
5. *Lit2Go* (audio books): http://etc.usf.edu/lit2go/index.htm
6. *Picture This! Teaching With Picture Books:*
   http://teachingwithpicturebooks.wordpress.com/

Clicker systems: These systems provide each student in a class with a wireless device that allows them to respond to a question the teacher has posed. Clickers are used on the TV show Millionaire! Contestants sometimes ask for audience input on the correct answer to a question, and after they respond, the percentage of people responding A, B, C, or D pops up next to the choices. Teachers might use these clickers to check for comprehension or as a review game. The benefit is that the teacher and students receive instant feedback. Google "clicker system" to find out more.

Creative Commons: (http://creativecommons.org/) provides a way for writers, artists, musicians, photographers and others to license their work for use by others. The website describes their licensing procedures as follows, "…you keep your copyright but allow people to copy and distribute your work provided they give you credit—and only on the conditions you specify." Helping students understand intellectual property rights, copyright issues, and the use of proper citation is much more complex than it was 10-20 years ago. People download images and audio files improperly every day and reuse them in presentations. By teaching students to look for material with Creative Commons licensing, and then to use it with the appropriate attribution, you help them to become responsible and ethical users of material available on the Web.

Flickr: (http://www.flickr.com/creativecommons/), a great site for images, also has a good section focusing on Creative Commons licensing. There is a helpful webcast archived at *Maine121* entitled "Fair Use and Media: From Copyright to Creative Commons" (http://maine121.org/webcasts-2/archives/digital-citizenship/) that will give you even more detailed information on this important topic. Finally, don't forget to check with your school librarian, your local expert on all things related to copyright rules including Creative Commons.

Dragon Dictate is a free smart phone and iPad app that allows a person to record his voice and then the app turns it into text. That text can be cut and pasted into an e-mail from the phone and sent to a device that has word processing capability. There, it can be pasted into a word processing document to be revised and edited. When using an iPad, you can skip the e-mail step and just cut and paste the text into a word processing document. This app does not work on all devices. Voice-to-text apps like Dragon Dictate have several uses in the classroom:

- Students with language disabilities related to expressing their ideas in writing can initially dictate their thoughts and then work with them in a word processing document with spelling and grammar support.
- While on field trips or in lab situations, students can record their observations.
- ELL students can practice their pronunciation and get immediate feedback with the text translation.

There is also a Dragon Search app that allows you to search the Internet by simply dictating the search term. A list of sites will come up in Google.

eBooks and iBooks are created to be read on eReaders like the Kindle, the Nook or the iPad. Some eBooks are simply print books that have been digitized. Project Gutenberg (www.gutenberg.com/) has a collection of over 38,000 digitized books free to download. Other eBooks are written just for the digital world and make use of links to add an interactive component to the text. An example is Al Gore's *Our Choice*, a five-dollar app for iPhones, iPods, and iPads. It contains videos, charts that break down into mini-sub charts, and images that with a touch of the finger expand to fill the screen. iBooks are simply an Apple product of the same nature. Apple will be publishing textbooks in an iBook format and making them available through iBooks on iTunes. Teachers and students are beginning to create their own eBooks with apps such as Book Creator for iPad and 3D Issue.

Foldables®: Dinah Zike (http://www.dinah.com/) has created a series of kinesthetic graphic organizers. They are actually manipulatives that students make by folding and cutting paper or oaktag. Compare and contrast, cause and effect, and vocabulary reviews are just some of the foldables currently used K-12 around the country.

Font size: Sometimes the size of the print in an article is a detriment to reading. Many middle grade students are frustrated by small print, while others have vision issues that are exacerbated by size 10 or 12 font (size of the type). Manipulating the size of the font is one of the easiest ways to accommodate learners with these issues. Word processing documents, websites, and pdf documents all can have their text enlarged to make the information more accessible. The method of enlarging the text varies depending on the type of document and the computer. Ask students for help—they will know how to make the changes.

Google Docs (http://www.google.com/google-d-s/b1.html) is a free online site that allows you to create and share documents, spreadsheets, presentations, and forms. Two or more people can work on the document at the same time and see each other's writing in real time. They do have to be in different sections of the document. To use it you need a Google account that gives you Gmail, a free email site. Here are a couple of examples how it might be used.

- A student writes a piece and shares it with his teacher for feedback. The teacher makes the comments digitally on the piece, and the student sees them immediately. The process becomes paperless once everyone gives up the need to print out copies. After multiple revisions, the student shares the piece with the entire class (and perhaps the world) via a Google folder.
- Two students work on a presentation together from their individual homes.
- The teacher posts a prompt and everyone in the class responds. The document is flashed on the screen with a LCD projector so everyone can see the comments.

Breaking the habit of printing out hard copies is difficult for many people. If I may share my personal journey on this subject: when I wrote my first book, I printed out every revision, made more revisions by hand, and typed them into the document, so I have multiple hard copy versions of *Everyone's Invited!* That was a tedious process, and one I vowed to give up. So I just stopped printing and buying reams of paper at Staples. I submit my manuscripts digitally, the feedback comes to me digitally, and I revise digitally. Using the *text-to-speech* application on my computer, I listen to what I've written, make more revisions, and submit my new version digitally. I back up regularly so my writing is saved in two places. I did not print out even one version of my second book or this one. Because all the versions of the book are on my computer, I can easily track my process. Google Docs provides teachers and students the same opportunity. There is no question that if I was still teaching writing, I would be using Google Docs and not hauling home heavy totes of papers to read and comment on by hand!

Google Earth: The satellite imagery used in this free download to any computer allows us to travel anywhere in the world instantaneously (http://www.google.com/earth/index.html). Studying Ancient Egypt? Take your students to Giza and gaze down on the Great Pyramid of Khufu. Not only can students see the setting of the places they are studying in relation to one another (e.g., where is the Sphinx in relation to the pyramid?), they can click on photos and add multiple layers to the image to see borders and other interesting features of the area.

Figure Appendix1 Screen shot of Google Earth image of Giza and its 3 pyramids (February 20, 2012)

Inquiry questions: Sometimes called essential questions, inquiry questions direct students' research and studies. They should be open-ended, not answerable in a few words, and require students to explore multiple resources to construct a response that requires them to use higher level thinking skills. Some may not have one answer and compel students to takes a stand and defend it with evidence. Some good sites to check out include:

- The Question Mark: http://questioning.org/mar05/essential.html
- Grant Wiggins' article, "What Is an Essential Question": http://www.authenticeducation.org/ae_bigideas/article.lasso?artid=53

LCD projector: LCD stands for liquid crystal display. The projector is one that hooks up to a computer and projects the monitor screen image onto a large viewing screen. Every teacher that has at least one computer in her classroom needs to have an LCD projector in the room for sharing Internet sites, modeling processes, showing videos, connecting to experts via Skype, and allowing students to share their work.

Likert Scale: Survey questions often require the respondents to place their answers somewhere along a continuum or rating scale. The continuum might start at *Strongly Disagree* and end at *Strongly Agree*.

Strongly Disagree	Disagree	Neither Agree or Disagree	Agree	Strongly Agree

Photo Booth is a fun application on Macs that has lots of classroom uses. Think about the "photo booth" at the amusement park or arcade that you and your friends squeezed into to take silly pictures. That's the idea behind this application, only you can take both stills and video with your computer camera! See the example on the next page of photos students took of their pottery.

The camera is located at the top of screen, and when you click on the circle icon of the camera, you get a 3-2-1 countdown before the image is snapped. Students can document all sorts of things with this application to help them demonstrate their learning (e.g. making a video to demonstrate their thinking as they work through a math problem or how well they have mastered their Spanish vocabulary).

Figure Appendix 2 *Students use the Photo Booth application to take pictures of their pottery to include in their portfolios.*

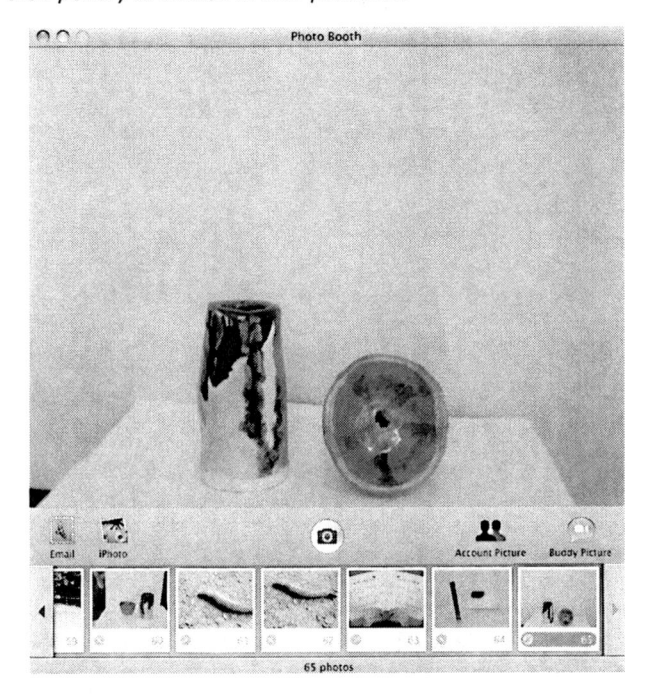

Podcasts seem to be available on almost every topic. Figure Appendix 3 on the following page lists some places to start looking for ones that might be useful in your classroom.

Making your own podcasts

- On a Mac: The Garage Band application is designed to allow users to create podcasts very easily. It is possible to record your voice, add images or video, and incorporate music. Garage Band has jingles that can be embedded into the podcast. The podcasts can be exported in a MP3 file that then can be uploaded to the Internet and shared.
- PCs: Many people use Audacity (http://audacity.sourceforge.net/) to create podcasts. There is a lot of information on the Internet on how to make your own using this application.
- If you are unsure about making podcasts by yourself, ask your students. If they do not already know how, they will figure it out at home or in the school lab and then teach you. Today's students rarely need an adult to show them how to use digital tools; they are experimenting with and sharing knowledge about digital devices and their applications all of the time.

Figure Appendix 3 *Sites for useful classroom podcasts*

Curriculum Area	Site
Arts–Visual and Performing	*Podcasts for Educators* (iTunes U): http://www.apple.com/education/itunes-u/ *Museum of Modern Art* (for kids): http://www.moma.org/visit/plan/atthemuseum/momaaudio
Language Arts	*10 Podcasts for Teachers and Kids:* http://www.scholastic.com/teachers/article/10-podcasts-teachers-and-kids *Princeton Review Vocab Minute:* http://www.learnoutloud.com/Podcast-Directory/Languages/Vocabulary-Building *Grammar Girl* http://grammar.quickanddirtytips.com/ WillowWeb #16 on 6 Traits Writing: http://itunes.apple.com/us/podcast/radio-willowweb/id73800253
Math	*Podcasts for Math* (multiple sites): http://techchef4u.wordpress.com/2011/05/17/podcasts-4-math/
Science	*Podcasts for Educators* (iTunes U): http://www.apple.com/education/itunes-u/ *10 Podcasts for Teachers and Kids:* http://www.scholastic.com/teachers/article/10-podcasts-teachers-and-kids *Science Friday:* http://sciencefriday.com/
Social Studies	*Humanities* Podcasts for Educators (iTunes U): http://www.apple.com/education/itunes-u/ *Top 20 History Podcasts:* http://www.onlinedegrees.org/top-20-history-podcasts/ *Kids.gov:* http://www.kids.gov
Technology	*KidFriday:* http://kidfriday.com/
Wellness	Kidtastics from Center for Disease Control: http://www2c.cdc.gov/podcasts/browse.asp?exactMatch=1&topic=Kidtastics DiscoveryHealth; http://www.discovery.com/radio/podcasts.html
World Languages	Kidtastics from Center for Disease Control: http://www2c.cdc.gov/podcasts/browse.asp?exactMatch=1&topic=Kidtastics (Some of the podcasts are in Spanish.) *Top 50 Podcasts for Learning a Foreign Language:* http://www.onlinedegrees.org/top-50-podcasts-for-learning-a-foreign-language/

Popplet and other Web-based webbing tools: There are several free online webbing tools including Popplet (http://popplet.com/) and Bubbl.us (https://bubbl.us/). Both are free and allow students to create colorful webs to use as study guides or as plans for essays or to take notes from a text. Popplet has an additional feature that allows the originator to send invites to others to participate via email. Students would be able to collaborate on creating a web with Popplet from any computer with Internet access.

Portaportal: This site (http://www.portaportal.com/) allows you to bookmark and post in one place multiple sites students might visit. The links, vetted by you, can be organized by topic. A site like Portaportal eliminates the need to type in lengthy URL addresses and thus saves time and frustration. The Portaportal site does not depend on the school server, so you can create it at home and have it online for students the next day. Students can create their own portaportals to save and share useful links for a research project. Another similar site is Delicious (http://delicious.com/). Search "social book marking" and a long list will pop up.

Stickies: Another fabulous free app that works across computer platforms is Stickies (http://www.zhornsoftware.co.uk/stickies/). They look like sticky notes; come in different colors; and are great for jotting down notes, quotes, and URLs. It is possible to make them float over a word processing document, thus providing notes on words and ideas to be included in the text.

Survey Tools Sites like Survey Monkey (www.surveymonkey.com) and Zoomerang (http://www.zoomerang.com) provide you and your students with tools to conduct free online surveys. Students can collect their own data to analyze for projects, you can assess background information about your students, or parents can be canvassed for their opinions on a topic. Surveys can include different types of questions such as open-ended and multiple choice, and once the responses are tabulated, the results are displayed in charts and graphs. Limitations to the free versions include the number of respondent answers allowed. All of the sites also have more complex options requiring payment. The next page shows an example of data reporting you can expect from a free tool.

Figure Appendix 4 Example of an online survey

1. I read			
books		6	40%
websites		3	20%
newspapers		0	0%
email		2	13%
texts		4	27%
	Total	15	100%

2. I read for pleasure			
every day for at least an hour		6	40%
several times a week		4	27%
rarely		5	33%
	Total	15	100%

3. Reading school assignments			
usually causes me no problems		7	47%
sometimes I struggle with reading assignments		4	27%
is something I avoid doing because I get frustrated		4	27%
	Total	15	100%

Think Alouds make the thinking and reading process transparent to students. Too many students do not have command of the necessary strategies to navigate complex text. You "think aloud" about text to show students how they might approach the assignment. By modeling behaviors of good thinkers, you provide interactive experiences for students that show them how to approach reading challenges. Some of the strategies that you might focus on include:

- using prior knowledge to make inferences and connect new information to what is already known
- asking questions
- visualizing
- summarizing
- synthesizing material from several sources
- self-monitoring and using strategies to help a student independently figure out what to do when confused by a particular passage

Process for Think Aloud:

- Choose your text and decide on your purpose (e.g., model a new process, help students navigate a particularly tricky part of the text, access prior knowledge and build enthusiasm).
- Read aloud the beginning of the text, then think out loud. Describe how you are processing the text. Read a bit more; and continue your thinking out loud.
- Read aloud another chunk of text and invite students to participate.
- Have students finish reading independently and then check for comprehension.

Think-Pair-Share is a strategy for any occasion! A powerful and effective strategy to use on a regular basis, it involves learners directly in the activity, and, because it is a paired activity, everyone in the room participates. Here are three reasons to use this strategy:

1. It is so versatile that it can be used as a before, during, or after reading/viewing/listening activity.
2. It incorporates elements of strategies that have been shown to be effective in increasing learning:
   - summarizing
   - comparing-contrasting
   - restating an idea in a new way
   - collaboration
   - think time
   - using different learning modalities
3. The same processes that increase understanding can be delivered in a variety of formats so that Think-Pair-Share can be adapted for different content areas, age groups, or energy levels.

Steps in the Think-Pair-Share process are:
1. Teacher asks a question or provides a prompt.
2. Students are given time to think about their individual responses.
3. Students pair up and discuss their responses.
4. Student pairs share their ideas with a larger group.

There are multiple ways to implement this strategy:

Examples of ways for pairs of students to THINK about things:

- How are things alike? Students look for similarities between items, events or ideas. *How are fractions and decimals alike?*

- How are things different? Students look for differences between items, events, or ideas. *How were the American Revolution and the French Revolution different?*

- How do things look different from the inside than from the outside? Students imagine what it would be like to be an observer inside or outside an item, event, system, etc. *You are a foreign entity floating along the circulatory system and are about to be attacked by white blood cells. Tell us what is happening to you.*

- What is your estimate or prediction? Students must make an educated guess or an inference using given information and their own general background knowledge. *If another huge Pacific Rim volcano erupted and spewed so much ash into the atmosphere that the sun was only half as bright, how would we be impacted here in New England?*

Examples of PROCESSES for pairs of students to use:

- Devil's advocate: students respond to their partner's point of view by taking the opposite view. *Respond to your partner's summary of the Boston Massacre by explaining what a British soldier would think about this event.*

- Tell/Add on: partner # 1 starts the discussion and then partner # 2 adds on to the story or information. *Another cause of the Civil War was...*

- Interview: Partners interview one another to find out what each other is thinking. Roles can be assumed. *So General Pickett, what were you thinking when you ordered your men to charge?*

- Act: partners act out the response. *First create an equilateral triangle, and then make the shape of an isosceles triangle.*

Examples of ways for partners to SHARE their thinking:

- Chart: each set of partners makes a chart and posts it. Class members walk around looking at the charts. You might want to give students the opportunity to write pertinent comments, observations, or questions on the charts as they walk around. When everyone returns to their seats, ask the students to reflect on what they have seen:

- What similarities do you see?
- What surprised you?
- Which of our questions have been answered?
- What new questions do we have?

- Chalk talk: post a big piece of mural paper in the front of the room with the prompt written on it. Give students chalk or markers to represent their thinking in a graphic way. Process using the questions above.
- Partners pair up with another pair; the four share their ideas: ask each group to choose one or two ideas to share with the entire class. Chart and discuss.
- Mini white boards: partners write their answers on the white board and at a given signal hold up their responses. iPads have an app called *Show Me Interactive White Board*—if you have access to iPads, check out this app!

Many of these ideas were inspired by Kagan's Think-Pair-Share Smart Card: www.KaganOnline.com

Think-Write-Pair-Share is a variation of Think-Pair-Share that adds writing to the activity.

1. The teacher first poses a problem, question, or something else to stimulate a response.
2. Learners think about their responses.
3. In Think-Write-Pair-Share, learners write or draw their ideas.
4. In pairs, learners share their thoughts/responses.
5. In the larger group, learners share their "best" ideas.

Total Physical Response: Dr. James Asher developed a teaching method for helping students to learn second languages called Total Physical Response (TPR). Movement is used to help students learn vocabulary and to practice conversations. An example might be using repetitive hand and feet motions in connection with counting 1-20 in the second language. The physical aspect of the lesson helps the learner internalize the new vocabulary.

YouTube: (http://www.youtube.com/), School Tube (http://www.schooltube.com/), and TeacherTube (http://www.teachertube.com/) are fantastic sources of video on just about anything. Want to learn how to teach inductive thinking? Search TeacherTube. Want to find a video explaining how to solve quadratic equations for your students to reference at home? Go to YouTube. A caution—the quality of the videos is not equal, so be sure to preview anything you recommend to students.

Twitter: If you can write a message in 140 characters or less, you are ready to "Tweet" on Twitter (http://twitter.com/). It's a free social networking tool that people in all walks of life are using to communicate, philosophize, and organize. Teachers are beginning to use Twitter to send students study questions, new vocabulary, and reminders.

Wikis are collaborative, online workspaces. Multiple people can read, write, and edit the same text. Plus, images, videos, and links can be added to the wiki. A wiki can have multiple pages all connected with links.

FAQs about wikis

1. *Are wikis costly?* For classroom use, the free wikis work just fine. Students will need email addresses. Many schools now provide email accounts for students, or they can sign up for free ones from home at Gmail or Hotmail. They only need the email address to register for the wiki site and to receive the initial invitation to join the wiki. After that, they can access the wiki from any computer with an Internet connection as long as they remember their passwords.

2. *How can I ensure that a wiki is a safe space for my students to work in?* When you start a wiki, you become the administrator of the wiki.

    - Using settings you control who can read, write, and edit the wiki. For example, if you want only your class to be able to see the wiki, you allow only invited people to access the wiki by listing their names and email addresses. No one else would be able to see the wiki.

    - You may decide that students can read and write in the wiki but not edit or change what others have already written. Or, if your purpose for having the wiki is to encourage collaborative writing, you may also give them editing privileges.

3. *Why would I use a wiki in my classroom?* Students can access wikis 24/7 from any computer with an Internet connection, so they always have the information in the wiki at their fingertips. They also allow students to work collaboratively during and after school. Furthermore, the information shows up instantaneously, so everyone has access to what is being said. If only one person is working on the wiki and it is being flashed on the screen via an LCD projector, everyone sees the changes at the

same time. If students are working on the wiki from their own computers, they will need to hit the refresh buttons to see the changes. In the classroom, a wiki might be used as:

- A workspace for students to respond to a reading or video. They can respond to a teacher-provided prompt and to one another's ideas. This scenario works best when each student is working at his or her own computer whether it is in the lab or on a laptop brought into the room on a cart. However, if you and your students only have access to a limited bank of computers, then you must orchestrate a way for each student to rotate through the class computers at the the back of the room.
- A place to share resources that will be helpful to students in their work. When you set up the wiki, you would include a page labeled "Resources." On that page you would list Internet resources, each with a live link out to the Web. Students would simply click on the link they wanted to explore. As new resources are discovered, the resource page could be updated continuously. Live links will appear underlined and in a different color in a wiki.
- A gallery of rubrics and exemplars of students' work so that both students and parents can examine what it means to meet the standard.
- A storage area for small groups working on a project. Resources, notes, links, or a project outline can be stored in a safe place that students can access from school or home. Using a wiki means things are less likely to get lost in the bottomless pit of a middle grades backpack!
- A gathering space for digital Exit Slips at the end of class.

4. *What is a class wiki?* A class wiki is one you set up as a part of your instructional plan for the lesson or unit. Everyone in your class and perhaps their parents have access to it. You might use it simply to post the unit components and deadlines so that general information is readily available, or it might be an integral and interactive component of the learning with students using it regularly in their work.

5. *Wikis sound intriguing, but I am really a neophyte when it comes to integrating technology in my instruction. Does it make sense for me to use wikis, or should I wait until I am more proficient with technology?* Start now, start small! Wikis like PBWorks (http://pbworks.com/education) give you step-by-step directions. Begin by just posting information, and practice making different pages that include links and images. Remember: you have a class full of digital natives who would love to help you out! Use students' expertise and willingness to figure out how to do things digitally. There is also an online article in the School Library

Journal entitled "Which wiki is right for you?" (http://www.schoollibraryjournal.com/article/CA6438167.html) that you might find useful. Finally, here is a wiki written by a teacher to explain how and why he uses wikis in his classroom: http://digitallyspeaking.pbworks.com/w/page/17791586/Wikis.

Word Walls: Once thought of as an elementary school strategy, word walls are now used nationally by secondary teachers with great success. Here's how to start using them:

- Identify key words in a unit and other important academic words critical to building a broad vocabulary.
- List them on a chart and post the chart in the classroom.
- Teach students to reference them when writing and speaking.
- Play games with them. Chapter 8 in *Everyone's Invited! Interactive Strategies That Engage Young Adolescent* by J. Spencer (2008), NMSA, has some specific examples.
- Point to them when teaching, so that ELL students and others see and hear the word together.
- Use them as a sponge activity at the beginning or ending of the class.
- Use them to review and summarize information.
- Use them as a modification for students with speech and language retrieval issues. The words are posted for students' reference when writing.

Make word walls interactive. It doesn't do any good just to post charts around the room and never refer to them.

- **Everyone one up:** *Raise your hand. When I call on you, tell me the definition of one of these words.*
- **First one out the door:** *Raise your hand. If I call on you and you use one of our words in a sentence, you can be the first one in line to leave for lunch!*
- **Review and summarize** information.
    - *Ella, can you tell us how decimals and fractions are related?*
    - *Zack, please compare and contrast mitosis and meiosis.*
- **Use pop culture** to provide students practice with words in different contexts. For example, think of the words "investigate," "integrity," and "reside." Then,

- *Find a character in a video or online game who shows integrity when faced with difficult situations.*
- *Find some characters on TV who investigate people or events.*
- *Think of a character in a movie who resides in a warm climate.*

- **Use sentence stems** that require students to demonstrate their understanding of a word by finishing the sentence:
    - *Meghan shows a positive attitude when she…*
    - *I would like to acquire a…*

- **Create a scenario** by connecting vocabulary words in sentences or questions and have students respond:
    - *How might we evaluate the impact of the new rules on the environment?*
    - *Would you prohibit the use of insecticides in fields near reservoirs?*

Wordle: Word clouds display text in interesting arrangements that capture the viewer's attention. Wordle (http://www.wordle.net/) is a free site where the user types in text, and the site creates a word cloud from those words. The user can change colors and organizational patterns until a pleasing word cloud emerges. If words are repeated in the text, they appear bigger than the surrounding ones. Below is a word cloud created at Wordle.net using the text of Lincoln's Gettysburg Address.

Figure Appendix 4 Example of a Word Cloud

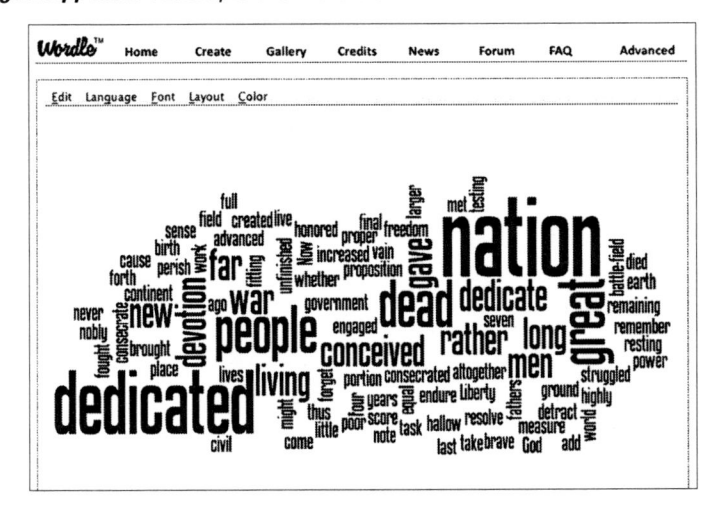

Appendix 147

References

About UDL. (n.d.). Retrieved from http://www.cast.org/udl/index.html

Allen, J. (1999). *Words, words, words.* Portland, ME: Stenhouse.

Armstrong, T. (2009). *Multiple intelligences in the classroom* (3rd ed.). [e-Reader version]. Retrieved from http://www.ascd.org/publications/books/109007/chapters/MI-Theory-and-Its-Critics.aspx

Bransford, J., Brown, A., & Cocking, S. (2006). *How people learn: Brain, mind, experience, and school.* Washington, DC: National Academy Press.

Christen, W., & Murphy, T. (1991). Increasing comprehension by activating prior knowledge. ED328885. Bloomington, IN: ERIC Clearinghouse on Reading and Communication Skill. Retrieved from http://www.ericdigests.org/pre-9219/prior.html

Cleveland, K. (2011). *Teaching boys who struggle in school: Strategies that turn underachievers into successful learners.* Alexandria, VA: Association for Supervision and Curriculum Development.

Cuban, L. (2012). Standards vs. customization: Finding the balance. *Educational Leadership. 69*(5), 10–15.

Dunn, R. (1990). Rita Dunn answers questions on learning styles. *Educational Leadership, 48*(2), 15–19.

Eliot, L. (2010). The myth of pink and blue brains. *Educational Leadership, 68*(3), 32–36.

Elliot, L. (2011). *Teach like a techie.* Peterborough, NH: Crystal Spring Books.

Gurian, M., with Stevens, K. (2011). *Boys & girls learn differently: A guide for teachers and parents.* [e-Reader version]. Retrieved from http://www.amazon.com/Girls-Differently-Teachers-Parents-ebook/dp/B0041G6SP0/ref=sr_1_1?s=digital-text&ie=UTF8&qid=1329940809&sr=1-1

Intellectual Development. *Mass General Hospital for Children.* Retrieved from http://www.massgeneral.org/children/adolescenthealth/articles/aa_intellectual_development.aspx

Jenkins, S. (1998). *Hottest, coldest, highest, deepest.* New York: Houghton Mifflin.

Kids Music Planet Podcast. Retrieved from http://kidsmusicplanet.blogspot.com/

King, K., Gurian, M., & Stevens, K. (2010). Gender-Friendly Schools. *Educational Leadership, 68*, 38-42.

Learn Out Loud. (Producer). (2012, February 18). *Road to Revolution: 1775—Great Moments in History* [Podiobook]. Retrieved from http://www.learnoutloud.com/podcaststream/listen.php?url=http://www.podiobooks.com/bookfeed/sampler/80/book.xml&all=1&title=20106

Lionni, L. (1963). *Swimmy.* New York: Knopf.

Maine Center for Meaningful Engaged Learning. (n.d.) Meaningful engaged learning. Retrieved from http://www.mcmel.org/web/Home.html

Maine Learning Results. (2008). *Science and technology.* Retrieved from http://www.maine.gov/education/lres/content.html

Marzano. R. (2004). *Building background information for academic achievement: Research on what works in schools.* Alexandria, VA: Association for Supervision and Curriculum Development.

McCully, E. (1996). *The bobbin girl.* New York: Dial Books.

Paterson, K. (1991). *Lyddie.* New York: Puffin.

Seasonal Dark Streaks on Mars. *Astronomy Picture of the Day.* Retrieved from http://apod.nasa.gov/apod/astropix.html

Spencer, J. (2008). *Everyone's invited! Interactive strategies that engage young adolescents.* Westerville, OH: National Middle School Association.

Squire, L. (2007). Learning and memory. *The Dana Guide to Brain Health.* [Electronic Version.] Section B13. Retrieved from http://www.dana.org/news/brainhealth/detail.aspx?id=10020

Tomlinson, C.A., and Eidson, C.C. (2003). *Differentiation in practice: A resource guide for differentiating curriculum.* Alexandria, VA: Association for Supervision and Curriculum Development.

Trend Data for Teens. *Pew Research Center: Pew Internet and American Life Project.* Retrieved from http://www.pewinternet.org/Trend-Data-for-Teens/Online-Activites-Total.aspx

Van Der Stuyf, R. (2002). Scaffolding as a Teaching Strategy. Retrieved from: http://condor.admin.ccny.cuny.edu/~group4/Van%20Der%20Stuyf/Van%20Der%20Stuyf%20Paper.doc

Willingham, D. Do Visual, Auditory, and Kinesthetic Learners Need Visual, Auditory, and Kinesthetic Instruction? Ask a cognitive scientist. AFT. Retrieved from http://www.aft.org/newspubs/periodicals/ae/summer2005/willingham.cfm.